BEST OF THE BEST
COOKBOOK
RECIPES

The best recipes from the **25** *best cookbooks of the year*

FOOD&WINE

FOOD & WINE BEST OF THE BEST VOL. 13

EDITOR **Kate Heddings**
DESIGN DIRECTOR **Patricia Sanchez, Nice Kern, LLC**
SENIOR EDITOR **Zoe Singer**
ASSOCIATE FOOD EDITOR **Melissa Rubel Jacobson**
CONTRIBUTING EDITOR **Jane Sigal**
ASSISTANT WINE EDITOR **Megan Krigbaum**
COPY EDITOR **Lisa Leventer**
DEPUTY PHOTO EDITOR **Anthony LaSala**
PRODUCTION MANAGER **Matt Carson**

FOOD & WINE MAGAZINE

S.V.P./EDITOR IN CHIEF **Dana Cowin**
CREATIVE DIRECTOR **Stephen Scoble**
MANAGING EDITOR **Mary Ellen Ward**
EXECUTIVE EDITOR **Pamela Kaufman**
EXECUTIVE FOOD EDITOR **Tina Ujlaki**
ART DIRECTOR **Courtney Waddell Eckersley**
EXECUTIVE ONLINE EDITOR **Rebecca Bauer**

AMERICAN EXPRESS PUBLISHING CORPORATION

PRESIDENT/C.E.O. **Ed Kelly**
CHIEF MARKETING OFFICER & PRESIDENT, DIGITAL MEDIA **Mark V. Stanich**
S.V.P./CHIEF FINANCIAL OFFICER **Paul B. Francis**
V.P./GENERAL MANAGERS **Frank Bland, Keith Strohmeier**

V.P., BOOKS & PRODUCTS/PUBLISHER **Marshall Corey**
DIRECTOR, BOOK PROGRAMS **Bruce Spanier**
SENIOR MARKETING MANAGER, BRANDED BOOKS **Eric Lucie**
ASSISTANT MARKETING MANAGER **Lizabeth Clark**
DIRECTOR OF FULFILLMENT & PREMIUM VALUE **Phil Black**
MANAGER OF CUSTOMER EXPERIENCE & PRODUCT DEVELOPMENT **Charles Graver**
DIRECTOR OF FINANCE **Thomas Noonan**
ASSOCIATE BUSINESS MANAGER **Uma Mahabir**
OPERATIONS DIRECTOR (PREPRESS) **Rosalie Abatemarco Samat**
OPERATIONS DIRECTOR (MANUFACTURING) **Anthony White**

FRONT AND BACK COVERS

PHOTOGRAPHER **Tina Rupp**
FOOD STYLIST **Alison Attenborough**
STYLE EDITOR **Jessica Romm**

INSIDE FLAP

PORTRAITS PHOTOGRAPHER **Andrew French**

ISBN 10: 1-60320-157-2
ISBN 13: 978-1-60320-157-5
ISSN 1524-2862

Published by American Express Publishing Corporation
1120 Avenue of the Americas, New York, New York 10036

Manufactured in the United States of America

BEST OF THE BEST
COOKBOOK
RECIPES

The best recipes from the 25 best cookbooks of the year

FOOD&WINE
BOOKS

American Express Publishing Corporation, New York

CONTENTS

Best of the Best Exclusives Recipe titles in **bold** are brand-new dishes appearing exclusively in *Best of the Best Cookbook Recipes.*

CONTENTS

Best of the Best Exclusives Recipe titles in **bold** are brand-new dishes appearing exclusively in *Best of the Best Cookbook Recipes.*

RECIPES

FOREWORD

Lately, more home cooks have been pushing themselves to ever-greater levels of mastery in the kitchen. Proof of this: the growing number of classes for anyone interested in learning how to butcher meat at home, or how to make cheese or sausage. There are even classes for people who want to brew their own kombucha! We're pleased to say that the cookbooks we feature in this year's *Best of the Best Cookbook Recipes* offer a terrific (and relatively inexpensive) way for any home cook to become more accomplished—without setting foot in a classroom.

In some of these books, the teacher is a chef, like Marco Canora of New York City's wonderful Italian restaurants Hearth and Terroir, who peppers his *Salt to Taste* with lots of tips and explanations. *Simply Mexican*, by professional cooking teacher Lourdes Castro, is so full of pointers that it will help anyone conquer the basics. Paula Wolfert's *Mediterranean Clay Pot Cooking* and Eileen Yin-Fei Lo's *Mastering the Art of Chinese Cooking* are comprehensive guides that can take the cook from kindergarten to grad school.

As in previous years, you'll find the recipes reproduced here just as they appeared in the original cookbooks. You'll also see never-before-published bonus recipes from almost every author. These include some of the most delicious dishes in the book, like Argentine chef Francis Mallmann's beautiful salad of burnt figs with burrata cheese, almonds and arugula (p. 133). New to this year's edition are simple, accessible wine pairings and information on how to find the authors online via their websites or Facebook, and how to follow them on Twitter.

We hope *Best of the Best* provides you with an excellent education and helps you become an ever-better cook.

Editor in Chief
FOOD & WINE Magazine

Editor
FOOD & WINE Cookbooks

COMFORT FOOD

LEMON ICEBOX PIE, P. 16

DAMGOODSWEET

David Guas & Raquel Pelzel

Much has been written about New Orleans's savory foods, but cookbook authors have long ignored the city's pastries and sweets. Now pastry chef David Guas fries beignets, bakes éclairs and flips crêpes in this fun cookbook, travelogue and memoir. Guas reaches back to his boyhood in New Orleans for desserts like bread pudding (his version is chocolaty) and silky banana pudding topped with crispy vanilla-wafer crumbs. (New Orleans was long a major port of entry for bananas from Latin America, which explains creations like banana pudding and bananas Foster.) Guas even includes pronunciation guides (éclairs are EEE-claires) so readers can not only bake like a New Orleans native, they can sound like one, too.

Published by The Taunton Press, $25

This classic Southern pie has pitch-perfect lemon flavor. The recipe is supereasy, too, combining a graham-cracker crust and a filling that requires only three ingredients: condensed milk, lemon and egg yolks.

LEMON ICEBOX PIE

MAKES ONE 9-INCH PIE

FOR THE CRUST

- 14 whole graham crackers
- ¼ cup sugar
- ¼ teaspoon salt
- 6 tablespoons unsalted butter, melted and still warm

FOR THE FILLING

- Two 14-ounce cans condensed milk
- 1¼ cups strained lemon juice (from the 2 zested lemons below plus an additional 4 to 6)
- Zest of 2 lemons
- 8 large egg yolks

FOR THE CHANTILLY CREAM

- 2 cups heavy cream
- ½ teaspoon vanilla extract
- ¼ cup confectioners' sugar

Clancy's is a super neighborhood-type spot on Annunciation Street frequented by lots of locals, myself included. It's not a Galatoire's-like institution, but it has a loyal following nonetheless. It's intimate, with low ceilings, and has an amazing jovial vibe that always makes me feel right at home. In the ten years since I lived in New Orleans, I can't remember a trip back to the city that didn't include at least one dinner at Clancy's— and at that dinner, I always order the same things: the fried eggplant, the sweetbreads, and the lemon icebox pie. My wife and I always share dessert, and this is one of the few that we actually fight over. While we'll happily listen to the waiter's dessert specials, our mind is made up the second we walk through the door: lemon icebox. As for making this at home, it just doesn't get any easier. It's simple and quick, plus it keeps in the freezer for over a week; it's a great dessert to make ahead for a dinner party. For a creamy key lime pie–like texture, let it sit out for 10 or 15 minutes before slicing.

To make the crust

Heat the oven to 325°F. Break the graham crackers into small pieces and place in the bowl of a food processor along with the sugar and salt. Pulse 8 times, until the cracker crumbs are semi-fine (they shouldn't be powdery but not in large shards either) and the crackers and sugar are combined. Pour in the butter and pulse until the butter is blended in and the mixture isn't crumbly and holds its shape when you squeeze it, about twelve 1-second pulses. Transfer the crust to a 9-inch springform pan and push and press the crumb mixture into the bottom and two-thirds of the way up the sides of the pan. Use the bottom of a measuring cup to press the crust into place. Set aside.

To make the filling

Whisk the condensed milk with the lemon juice and set aside. Whisk the zest with the egg yolks in a medium bowl until pale, 30 to 60 seconds, and then whisk in the lemon juice–condensed milk mixture.

Place the springform pan on a rimmed baking sheet, pour the mixture into the crust, and carefully transfer the baking sheet to the oven. Bake until the center jiggles slightly, like a soft-setting custard, about 25 minutes. Remove from the oven and cool for 1 hour on a cooling rack. Loosely cover the pan with plastic wrap (be careful not to let the plastic wrap touch the top of the pie) and freeze for at least 6 hours or overnight.

To make the chantilly cream

Pour the heavy cream into the bowl of a stand mixer (or in a large bowl if using a hand mixer). Add the vanilla and sift in the confectioners' sugar. Whip on low speed to combine and then increase the speed to medium-high and whip until medium-stiff peaks form, about 1½ minutes.

Before serving, wrap a wet, warm kitchen towel around the edges of the springform pan to release the pie from the pan's sides. Unclasp the pan and remove the pie. Fill a pitcher with hot water, dunk your knife in, wipe off the blade, and slice. Top with a dollop of chantilly cream and serve immediately, or keep in the freezer for up to 1 week.

DAMGOODSWEET
David Guas & Raquel Pelzel

Bread puddings can be dry and dense, but the unusually high ratio of custard to bread in this recipe makes it creamy and genuinely pudding-like. The boozy caramel sauce is luxurious, too.

CHOCOLATE BREAD PUDDING WITH SALTED CARAMEL

SERVES 10 TO 12

FOR THE BREAD PUDDING
- 2 tablespoons unsalted butter, at room temperature
- 1 pound brioche bread, crust removed and sliced into 1-inch cubes
- 6 large eggs
- ⅓ cup Dutch-processed cocoa powder
- 12 ounces bittersweet chocolate (preferably 66 to 72 percent cacao), finely chopped
- 5½ cups whole milk
- 2½ cups heavy cream
- 1¾ cups sugar
- ¼ teaspoon salt
- ¾ teaspoon vanilla extract

FOR THE CARAMEL SAUCE
- 1½ cups sugar
- ¾ cup heavy cream
- 2 tablespoons unsalted butter, at room temperature
- ¼ cup bourbon
- ¼ teaspoon salt

AUTHOR'S NOTE

In New Orleans you'd make bread pudding with airy Leidenheimer French bread, but I find that brioche, challah, or even day-old croissants or king cake make for an outrageously decadent pudding (just don't tell your momma it ain't Leidenheimer!).

Bread pudding is one of my favorite holiday traditions, and I make it for my family every holiday season. It's great for large gatherings and potlucks because it can be made up to three days ahead of time. This chocolate version is amazing when served with salted bourbon caramel.

To make the pudding

Heat the oven to 325°F. Grease a 13-by-9-inch baking dish with the softened butter and set aside.

Place the bread cubes on a rimmed baking sheet and toast in the oven until golden-brown, 12 to 15 minutes, rotating midway through. Set aside to cool.

Place the bread in the prepared baking dish and set aside. Whisk the eggs in a medium bowl and set aside. Sift the cocoa into a medium bowl and set aside.

Place the chocolate in a large bowl. Bring the milk, cream, sugar, and salt to a boil in a large pot, stirring occasionally to dissolve the sugar. Turn off the heat, stir in the vanilla, and then pour the hot mixture over the chopped chocolate. Cover the bowl with plastic wrap, set aside for 5 minutes, and then whisk until smooth.

Whisk ½ cup of the chocolate mixture into the cocoa, stirring until smooth. Whisk in another ½ cup of the chocolate mixture and then whisk in the eggs. Transfer to the large bowl of remaining chocolate mixture and whisk until they are completely incorporated.

continued on p. 20

COMFORT FOOD

DAM GOOD SWEET
David Guas & Raquel Pelzel

AUTHOR'S NOTE

Bread pudding is one of those desserts that is great for entertaining because it can be made and refrigerated a few days ahead of time. To warm, reheat the entire pan of bread pudding in a water bath in a 350°F oven until the center is warm. Or, for individual portions, slice and reheat in your microwave or toaster oven. The caramel can be covered and stored at room temperature for 2 days, or covered and refrigerated for up to 2 weeks ahead of time. Reheat the sauce in a saucepan or in your microwave.

Pour all but 1 cup of the chocolate mixture over the bread cubes in the baking dish and set aside so the bread can soak up the liquid. Press down on the bread with a wooden spoon every 15 minutes for 1 hour, adding the rest of the chocolate mixture after about 30 minutes, or when the bread has soaked up enough so the last cup of liquid will fit.

Heat the oven to 350°F.

Cover the bread pudding with aluminum foil and use a paring knife to make 4 small slits in the foil to allow steam to escape. Set the baking dish in a large roasting pan and place in the oven. Pour enough hot water in the roasting pan so the water reaches 1 inch up the side of the baking dish (if you don't have a roasting pan large enough to fit the baking dish, set the dish onto a rimmed baking sheet and slide it in the oven, adding enough water to the baking sheet so it cushions the baking dish but doesn't spill over). Bake for 45 minutes, and then remove the foil and bake until the pudding begins to puff slightly and the center bounces back to light pressure, about another 25 to 35 minutes. Cool for 30 minutes.

To make the sauce

While the bread pudding cools, make the caramel. Place the sugar in a 2-quart saucepan and add ¼ cup of water. Cover (or if you can't find a lid, top the saucepan with a heatproof bowl, making sure the bottom of the bowl doesn't touch the sugar) and cook over medium heat, swirling the mixture every 1 to 2 minutes, until the sugar is liquefied, about 6 minutes. Continue to cook until the sugar is a medium-amber color, another 4 to 6 minutes. Turn off the heat and add the cream (it will vigorously bubble up at first), whisking the mixture until smooth, then add the softened butter, bourbon, and salt. Set aside and serve with the still-warm bread pudding.

One of the best parts of this pudding is the simple cookie-crumb topping: Guas crushes vanilla wafers, then tosses them with sugar, cinnamon and butter before baking them until they're crunchy.

BANANA PUDDING WITH VANILLA WAFER CRUMBLE

SERVES 6

FOR THE PUDDING
- 5 large egg yolks
- ½ cup sugar
- ¼ cup cornstarch
- ¼ teaspoon salt
- 2 cups whole milk
- 3 tablespoons banana liqueur (or 1 teaspoon banana flavoring)
- 2 teaspoons vanilla extract
- 2 tablespoons unsalted butter
- 2 ripe bananas

FOR THE CRUMBLE
- 1 cup vanilla wafers (about 15 cookies)
- 2 teaspoons sugar
- ¼ teaspoon ground cinnamon
- Pinch salt
- 1 tablespoon unsalted butter, melted

Funerals are a big deal in New Orleans and our family was no exception. Though we didn't send our beloveds off with a jazz funeral and a brass band, we did put out quite a spread to keep the mourners sated. I would sit through the eulogy, the whole time keeping my fingers crossed that I'd meet up with banana pudding at the post-service buffet table.

Sometimes it was layered with vanilla wafers like a parfait. Sometimes the cookies were half sunken into the abyss. Sometimes there were bananas and sometimes there weren't. I'd always scoop out a giant serving with more than my fair share of cookies. Now that I'm grown, I like my banana pudding flavored with banana liqueur and topped with a vanilla-wafer and cinnamon-tossed crumb topping. The topping always stays crisp and provides an amazing contrast to the soft-tender bite of the chopped bananas and the silkiness of the pudding. It's humble and homey but just different enough from the traditional version that I feel good about serving it in a more sophisticated setting.

To make the pudding

Whisk the egg yolks, sugar, cornstarch, and salt together in a medium bowl and set aside. Bring the milk to a boil in a medium saucepan. Remove from the heat and whisk a little at a time into the egg mixture. Once the bottom of the bowl is warm, slowly whisk in the remaining hot milk. Pour the mixture back into a clean medium saucepan (cleaning the saucepan prevents

continued on p. 23

the pudding from scorching), add the banana liqueur, and whisk over medium-low heat until it thickens, about 2 minutes. Cook while constantly whisking until the pudding is glossy and quite thick, 1½ to 2 minutes longer. Transfer the pudding to a clean bowl.

Add the vanilla and butter and gently whisk until the butter is completely melted and incorporated. Press a piece of plastic wrap onto the surface of the pudding to prevent a skin from forming. Refrigerate for 4 hours.

To make the crumble

While the pudding sets, heat the oven to 325°F. Line a rimmed baking sheet with parchment paper and set aside. Place the wafers in a resealable plastic bag and seal (make sure there is no air in the bag prior to sealing). Using a rolling pin or a flat-bottomed saucepan or pot, crush the vanilla wafers until they're coarsely ground. Transfer them to a small bowl and stir in the sugar, cinnamon, and salt. Use a spoon to evenly stir in the melted butter, transfer to the prepared baking sheet, and toast in the oven until brown and fragrant, 12 to 15 minutes. Remove from the oven and set aside to cool. (The crumbs can be stored in an airtight container for up to 5 days at room temperature or frozen for up to 2 months; re-crisp in a 325°F oven for 6 to 7 minutes if necessary.)

To serve

Slice the bananas in half crosswise and then slice in half lengthwise so you have 4 quarters. Slice the banana quarters crosswise into ½-inch pieces and divide between 6 custard cups or martini glasses (sprinkle with a squeeze of lemon juice if you like—this helps prevent browning). Whisk the pudding until it is soft and smooth, about 30 seconds, and then divide it between the custard cups. Top with the vanilla wafer mixture and serve. (If not served immediately, the pudding will keep in the refrigerator for up to 3 days, with plastic wrap intact. Sprinkle the crumbs on just before serving.)

DAMGOODSWEET
David Guas & Raquel Pelzel

Just-ground coffee beans give these silky custards intense flavor; brûléed demerara (raw sugar) creates a thick, crackling top.

CAFÉ AU LAIT CRÈME BRÛLÉE

SERVES 6

- 3 tablespoons French roast whole coffee beans
- 1¼ cups whole milk
- 1¼ cups heavy cream
- 6 tablespoons sugar
- 11 large egg yolks
- ⅛ teaspoon salt
- 6 teaspoons demerara sugar

AUTHOR'S NOTE

Make a modest investment in a handheld blowtorch (available at most every gourmet cookware shop) or even the big, durable propane tanks from your neighborhood hardware store so you can evenly caramelize the sugar topping quickly, keeping the custard nice and cool. If you have no other option, you can use the broiler to brûlée the sugar, but your custard will warm up a little in the process.

Heat the oven to 200°F. Place the coffee beans in a coffee grinder, pulse for two 1-second pulses (some beans may still be whole, which is okay), and set aside.

Stir the milk, cream, and sugar together in a medium saucepan and bring to a boil over medium-high heat. Turn the heat off, stir in the coffee beans, and let the mixture steep for 5 minutes.

Whisk the egg yolks and salt together in a large bowl. Vigorously whisk the steeped milk mixture into the egg yolks, then strain into a clean bowl. Place six 4-ounce ramekins (preferably shallow oval ramekins; see the equipment note below) on a rimmed baking sheet and evenly divide the custard mixture between them. Place the baking sheet in the oven and bake until a dime-size center portion of the custard gives a slight jiggle when the baking sheet is tapped, about 50 minutes to 1 hour. Let the custards cool at room temperature for 30 minutes before covering each with plastic wrap and refrigerating for at least 8 hours or up to 3 days.

Evenly sprinkle the top of each custard with 1 teaspoon of coarse demerara sugar (if you are using round ramekins, you may not use the full teaspoon) and brown it using a hand-held blowtorch. Serve immediately after brûléeing.

EQUIPMENT NOTE I like using shallow, oval-shaped ramekins to make crème brûlée because their long and shallow shape allows for a greater ratio of crisp sugar topping to custard.

This brownie has a gooey, nutty topping that evokes New Orleans's famous praline candy; it's like a brownie pecan pie.

CREOLE BROWNIES

MAKES 2 DOZEN BROWNIES

BROWNIES
1½ cups all-purpose flour
¼ cup unsweetened cocoa powder
9 ounces bittersweet chocolate (preferably 66 to 72 percent), coarsely chopped
2 sticks plus 2 tablespoons (9 ounces) unsalted butter, cut into 1-inch pieces
1¼ cups granulated sugar
3 large eggs
2 teaspoons pure vanilla extract
1 teaspoon kosher salt

PRALINE CARAMEL
1½ cups pecan halves
1 cup water
¼ cup honey
2 cups packed light brown sugar
¼ teaspoon kosher salt
½ teaspoon pure vanilla extract

1. Preheat the oven to 375°F. Line a 9-by-13-inch baking pan with parchment paper, leaving an overhang on the long sides.

2. Make the brownies: In a medium bowl, whisk the flour with the cocoa powder. In a heatproof medium bowl set over a saucepan of simmering water, combine the chocolate and butter and cook until softened. Remove from the heat and stir until fully melted.

3. In a large bowl, using an electric mixer, beat the granulated sugar with the eggs, vanilla and salt at high speed until pale and thick, about 2 minutes. Add the melted chocolate and beat at low speed for 1 minute. Using a spatula, fold in the flour mixture. Scrape the batter into the prepared pan and bake for about 18 minutes, until the brownies are just set and the surface is slightly cracked. Let cool. Lower the oven temperature to 350°F.

4. Make the praline caramel: Spread the pecans in a pie plate and toast for about 10 minutes, until fragrant and golden. Let cool, then coarsely chop the pecans. In a medium saucepan, mix the pecans with the water, honey, brown sugar and salt. Bring to a simmer and cook over moderate heat until the caramel is thick and dark, about 35 minutes. Remove from the heat and stir in the vanilla.

5. Pour the caramel over the brownies, spreading it in an even layer. Let cool until set, about 2 hours. Using the parchment paper overhang, lift the brownies out of the pan. Lightly spray a sharp knife with cooking spray before cutting the brownies.

MAKE AHEAD The brownies can be stored in an airtight container for up to 2 days.

DAVID GUAS ONLINE
damgoodsweet.com
David Guas
@damgoodsweet

BUTTERMILK FRIED CHICKEN, P. 28

AD HOC AT HOME

*Thomas Keller with Dave Cruz along with
Susie Heller, Michael Ruhlman & Amy Vogler*

Chefs always point to Thomas Keller's 1999 best seller, *The French Laundry Cookbook*—an in-depth look at one of the country's most innovative restaurants—as the model for the unapologetically complex books they want to write. But they should put down their tongs and take a look at this collection of family-style recipes from Ad Hoc, Keller's casual Napa Valley restaurant. It pairs Keller's famous precision (drain fried chicken skin side up) with practicality (date your spice jars) and accessibility (if the toothpick comes out wet when you test brownies, poke again; you may have hit a chocolate chip). While the book is directed at home cooks, even chefs might learn something, as when Keller says, "Step away from the tongs. Too often tongs crush or tear food."

Published by Artisan, $50

AD HOC AT HOME
Thomas Keller with Dave Cruz along with
Susie Heller, Michael Ruhlman & Amy Vogler

Never underestimate the benefit of brining, which gives this chicken its fantastic texture and flavor. Even leaving the chicken in the brine for half the suggested amount of time has an impact.

BUTTERMILK FRIED CHICKEN

SERVES 4 TO 6

Two 2½- to 3-pound chickens
    (see Author's Note below)
Chicken Brine (recipe follows), cold

FOR DREDGING AND FRYING
Peanut or canola oil for deep-frying
  1 quart buttermilk
Kosher salt and freshly ground
    black pepper

COATING
  6 cups all-purpose flour
  ¼ cup garlic powder
  ¼ cup onion powder
  1 tablespoon plus 1 teaspoon paprika
  1 tablespoon plus 1 teaspoon cayenne
  1 tablespoon plus 1 teaspoon kosher
    salt
  1 teaspoon freshly ground
    black pepper

Ground fleur de sel or fine sea salt
Rosemary and thyme sprigs for garnish

AUTHOR'S NOTE

You may need to go to a farmers' market to get small chickens. Grocery store chickens often run 3 to 4 pounds. They can be used in this recipe, but 2½- to 3-pound chickens are a little easier to cook at the temperatures we recommend and, most important, pieces this size result in the optimal meat-to-crust proportion.

Cut each chicken into 10 pieces: 2 legs, 2 thighs, 4 breast quarters, and 2 wings. Pour the brine into a container large enough to hold the chicken, add in the chicken, and refrigerate for 12 hours (no longer, or the chicken may become too salty).

Remove the chicken from the brine (discard the brine) and rinse under cold water, removing any herbs or spices sticking to the skin. Pat dry with paper towels, or let air-dry. Let rest at room temperature for 1½ hours, or until it comes to room temperature.

If you have two large pots (about 6 inches deep) and a lot of oil, you can cook the dark and white meat at the same time; if not, cook the dark meat first, then turn up the heat and cook the white meat. No matter what size pot you have, the oil should not come more than one-third of the way up the sides of the pot. Fill the pot with at least 2 inches of peanut oil and heat to 320°F. Set a cooling rack over a baking sheet. Line a second baking sheet with parchment paper. Meanwhile, combine all the coating ingredients in a large bowl. Transfer half the coating to a second large bowl. Pour the buttermilk into a third bowl and season with salt and pepper. Set up a dipping station: the chicken pieces, one bowl of coating, the bowl of buttermilk, the second bowl of coating, and the parchment-lined baking sheet.

Just before frying, dip the chicken thighs into the first bowl of coating, turning to coat and patting off the excess; dip them into the buttermilk, allowing the excess to run back into the bowl; then dip them into the second bowl of coating. Transfer to the parchment-lined pan. Carefully lower the thighs into the hot oil. Adjust the heat as necessary to return the oil to the

EDITOR'S WINE CHOICE

Focused, raspberry-scented Grenache: 2007 Unti

AUTHOR'S NOTE

We let the chicken rest for 7 to 10 minutes after it comes out of the fryer so that it has a chance to cool down. If the chicken has rested for longer than 10 minutes, put the tray of chicken in a 400°F oven for a minute or two to ensure that the crust is crisp and the chicken is hot.

MAKES 2 GALLONS

5	lemons, halved
12	bay leaves
1	bunch (4 ounces) flat-leaf parsley
1	bunch (1 ounce) thyme
½	cup clover honey
1	head garlic, halved through the equator
¾	cup black peppercorns
2	cups Diamond Crystal kosher salt
2	gallons water

proper temperature. Fry for 2 minutes, then carefully move the chicken pieces around in the oil and continue to fry, monitoring the oil temperature and turning the pieces as necessary for even cooking, for 11 to 12 minutes, until the chicken is a deep golden brown, cooked through, and very crisp. Meanwhile, coat the drumsticks and transfer to the parchment-lined pan.

Transfer the cooked thighs to the cooling rack skin side up and let rest while you fry the remaining chicken. (Putting the pieces skin side up will allow excess fat to drain, whereas leaving them skin side down could trap some of the fat.) Make sure that the oil is at the correct temperature, and cook the chicken drumsticks. When the drumsticks are done, lean them meat side up against the thighs to drain, then sprinkle the chicken with fine sea salt.

Turn up the heat and heat the oil to 340°F. Meanwhile, coat the chicken breasts and wings. Carefully lower the chicken breasts into the hot oil and fry for 7 minutes, or until golden brown, cooked through, and crisp. Transfer to the rack, sprinkle with salt, and turn skin side up. Cook the wings for 6 minutes, or until golden brown and cooked through. Transfer the wings to the rack and turn off the heat. Arrange the chicken on a serving platter. Add the herb sprigs to the oil (which will still be hot) and let them cook and crisp for a few seconds, then arrange them over the chicken.

CHICKEN BRINE

The key ingredient here is the lemon, which goes wonderfully with chicken, as do the herbs: bay leaf, parsley, and thyme. This amount of brine will be enough for 10 pounds. If using another brand of kosher salt, use exactly 10 ounces.

Combine all the ingredients in a large pot, cover, and bring to a boil. Boil for 1 minute, stirring to dissolve the salt. Remove from the heat and cool completely, then chill before using. The brine can be refrigerated for up to 3 days.

The pan sauce here, made with butter, wine, chicken stock and fresh tarragon, is divine and quick; starting with chicken cutlets instead of breasts makes the recipe faster yet.

SAUTÉED CHICKEN BREASTS WITH TARRAGON

SERVES 6

- 1 teaspoon sweet paprika
- 1 teaspoon yellow curry powder or Madras curry powder
- 6 large (about 6 ounces each) or 12 small (about 3 ounces each) boneless, skinless chicken breasts
- Kosher salt
- Canola oil
- 3 tablespoons (1½ ounces) unsalted butter
- 1 tablespoon minced shallot
- ¼ cup dry white wine, such as Sauvignon Blanc
- 1 cup Chicken Stock (recipe follows)
- 1 tablespoon coarsely chopped tarragon, plus 1 tablespoon tarragon leaves
- Freshly ground black pepper

A chicken breast—flattened, seasoned, sautéed, and served with a simple pan sauce—can be delicious and very easy to prepare. The curry brings a lot of flavor to the chicken, and the tarragon butter sauce blends beautifully with that flavor.

This basic method works with other lean, tender cuts of meat as well, such as pork loin or veal.

Mix together the paprika and curry in a small bowl. Season the chicken breasts on both sides with the mixture. Cover and refrigerate for 2 hours.

Lay 2 pieces of chicken on a large piece of plastic wrap, cover with a second piece of plastic wrap, and, using a meat pounder, pound to about ¼ inch thick. Transfer to a plate and repeat with the remaining chicken. (The chicken can be wrapped and refrigerated for up to 12 hours.)

Preheat the oven to 200°F. Set a cooling rack over a baking sheet.

Season the chicken on both sides with salt. Heat some canola oil in a large frying pan over medium-high heat. Working in batches, without crowding, add the chicken to the pan, presentation (smooth) side down, and cook, adjusting the heat if necessary, until the bottom is golden brown, 1 to 1½ minutes. Turn to the second side and cook until golden, another 1 to 1½ minutes. Transfer to the rack and keep warm in the oven. Add oil to the pan as needed as you cook the remaining chicken.

Pour any remaining oil from the pan and wipe out any burned bits. Melt 1 tablespoon of the butter over medium-high heat. Add the shallot to the pan, reduce the heat to medium, and cook for 30 seconds, swirling the pan to coat the shallot with

EDITOR'S WINE CHOICE

Full-bodied, peach-inflected Rhône-style white blend: 2008 Tablas Creek Côtes de Tablas Blanc

the butter. Pour in the wine, increase the heat to medium-high, and cook until the wine has reduced by half, about 1 minute. Add the chicken stock, bring to a boil, and cook until slightly reduced and thickened, 1 to 2 minutes. Stir in the chopped tarragon, the remaining 2 tablespoons butter, and any juices that have accumulated on the baking sheet and swirl to melt the butter. Season to taste with salt and pepper.

Arrange the chicken on a platter, pour the sauce over it, and garnish with the tarragon leaves.

CHICKEN STOCK

MAKES 4½ QUARTS

- 5 pounds chicken bones, necks, and backs
- 1 pound chicken feet (optional)
- About 4 quarts cold water
- About 8 cups ice cubes
- 1¾ cups carrots cut into 1-inch cubes
- 2 heaping cups leeks cut into 1-inch pieces (white and light green parts only)
- 1½ cups Spanish onions cut into 1-inch pieces
- 1 bay leaf

This is a very light stock, appropriate for a variety of uses—from the braising liquid for meats and beans to the base for soups and sauces. For a stronger chicken flavor, reduce the finished stock by one-third or use more bones.

As with all stocks, you're looking to remove impurities—fats and food particles—while extracting as much flavor and gelatin as possible from the bones, and the maximum flavor from the vegetables and aromatics. You do this not only through gentle heat, but through gradual heat transitions as well; in other words, you don't start with hot water, you begin with cold and bring it slowly up to heat. Skim often throughout the cooking process—especially in the beginning, when a lot of impurities will rise to the surface. You can't skim too much. I add ice cubes after the stock has come up to a simmer; this chills any remaining fat and makes it easier to remove. Maintain a gentle heat over a long time, continuing to skim, and then carefully strain the stock. All the steps are simple, but each one is essential.

Rinse the bones, necks, backs, and chicken feet, if using, thoroughly under cold water to remove all visible blood. Remove and discard any organs still attached to the bones. (Rinsing the bones and removing any organs is an essential

continued on p. 32

COMFORT FOOD

AD HOC AT HOME
Thomas Keller with Dave Cruz along with
Susie Heller, Michael Ruhlman & Amy Vogler

first step in the clarification of the stock, as this removes any blood proteins that would coagulate when heated and cloud the stock.)

Put all the bones and the feet, if using, in a very large stockpot and add 4 quarts cold water, or just enough to cover the bones. Set the pot to one side of the burner (see Author's Note). Slowly bring the liquid to a simmer, beginning to skim as soon as any impurities rise to the top. (It is important to keep skimming as the stock comes to a simmer, because impurities could otherwise be pulled back into the liquid and cloud the finished stock.) Once the liquid is at a simmer, add the ice cubes (ice will solidify the remaining fat and make it easier to remove), and then remove the fat. Skim off as much of the impurities as possible. (Once the vegetables have been added, skimming will be more difficult.)

Add the remaining ingredients; slowly bring the liquid back to a simmer, skimming frequently. Simmer for another 40 minutes, skimming often. Turn off the heat; let the stock rest for 10 minutes (this allows any particles to settle).

Prepare an ice bath. Set a fine-mesh conical strainer over a container large enough to hold at least 6 quarts liquid. Use a ladle to transfer the stock from the pot to the strainer. (It is important to ladle the stock rather than pour it, as the force of pouring it out all at once would carry impurities through the strainer.) Do not press on the solids in the strainer or force through any liquid, or the stock will be cloudy. Discard any stock that is cloudy with impurities at the bottom of the pot.

Measure the stock. If you have more than 4½ quarts, pour it into a saucepan, bring it to a simmer, and simmer to reduce. Strain into a clean container before measuring again.

Put the container in the ice bath to cool the stock rapidly. Stir occasionally until there are no longer any traces of steam and the stock is cool. Store in the refrigerator for up to 3 days, or freeze in smaller containers for up to 2 months.

This Leek Bread Pudding is custard-like and creamy and almost over-the-top rich. Opting for the Pullman sandwich loaf (white bread) over buttery brioche lightens the recipe a bit.

LEEK BREAD PUDDING

SERVES 12 AS A SIDE DISH,
6 TO 8 AS A MAIN COURSE

- 2 cups ½-inch-thick slices leeks (white and light green parts only)
- Kosher salt
- 4 tablespoons (2 ounces) unsalted butter
- Freshly ground black pepper
- 12 cups 1-inch cubes crustless brioche or Pullman sandwich loaf
- 1 tablespoon finely chopped chives
- 1 teaspoon thyme leaves
- 3 large eggs
- 3 cups whole milk
- 3 cups heavy cream
- Freshly grated nutmeg
- 1 cup shredded Comté or Emmentaler

Just as custards work well in the savory portion of the meal, although they're more often served as a dessert, so do bread puddings.

Preheat the oven to 350°F.

Put the leek rounds in a large bowl of tepid water and swish so that any dirt falls to the bottom of the bowl. Set a medium sauté pan over medium-high heat, lift the leeks from the water, drain, and add them to the pan. Season with salt and cook, stirring often, for about 5 minutes. As the leeks begin to soften, lower the heat to medium-low. The leeks will release liquid. Stir in the butter to emulsify, and season with pepper to taste. Cover the pan with a parchment lid, and cook, stirring every 10 minutes, until the leeks are very soft, 30 to 35 minutes. If at any point the butter breaks or looks oily, stir in about a tablespoon of water to re-emulsify the sauce. Remove and discard the parchment lid.

Meanwhile, spread the bread cubes on a baking sheet and toast in the oven for about 20 minutes, rotating the pan about halfway through, until dry and pale gold. Transfer to a large bowl. Leave the oven on.

Add the leeks to the bread and toss well, then add the chives and thyme.

continued on p. 35

AD HOC AT HOME
Thomas Keller with Dave Cruz along with
Susie Heller, Michael Ruhlman & Amy Vogler

**Fresh, zippy Pinot Grigio:
2009 Palmina**

Lightly whisk the eggs in another large bowl. Whisk in the milk, cream, a generous pinch of salt, pepper to taste, and a pinch of nutmeg.

Sprinkle ¼ cup of the cheese in the bottom of a 9-by-13-inch baking pan. Spread half the leeks and croutons in the pan and sprinkle with another ¼ cup cheese. Scatter the remaining leeks and croutons over and top with another ¼ cup cheese. Pour in enough of the custard mixture to cover the bread and press gently on the bread so it soaks in the milk. Let soak for about 15 minutes.

Add the remaining custard, allowing some of the soaked cubes of bread to protrude. Sprinkle the remaining ¼ cup cheese on top and sprinkle with salt.

Bake for 1½ hours, or until the pudding feels set and the top is brown and bubbling.

best of the best cookbook recipes | 35

The centers of Keller's exceptional brownies are so dense and the edges so crisp. The secret is butter: lots and lots of butter.

BROWNIES

MAKES 12 BROWNIES

- ¾ cup all-purpose flour
- 1 cup unsweetened alkalized cocoa powder
- 1 teaspoon kosher salt
- ¾ pound (3 sticks) unsalted butter, cut into 1-tablespoon pieces
- 3 large eggs
- 1¾ cups granulated sugar
- ½ teaspoon vanilla paste or pure vanilla extract
- 6 ounces 61 to 64 percent chocolate, chopped into chip-sized pieces (about 1½ cups)

Powdered sugar for dusting

Brownies embody so much of what I love about dessert generally—they remind me of family, comfort, childhood. They draw you to them. You can turn these into a special dessert by serving them alongside caramel ice cream or with vanilla ice cream and caramel sauce, but they're great with just a little whipped cream or powdered sugar—or all by themselves.

Preheat the oven to 350°F. We use a 9-inch square silicone mold, because it keeps the edges from overcooking; if you use a metal or glass baking pan, butter and flour it. Set aside.

Sift together the flour, cocoa powder, and salt; set aside.

Melt half the butter in a small saucepan over medium heat, stirring occasionally. Put the remaining butter in a medium bowl. Pour the melted butter over the bowl of butter and stir to melt the butter. The butter should look creamy, with small bits of unmelted butter, and be at room temperature.

In the bowl of a stand mixer fitted with the paddle, mix together the eggs and sugar on medium speed for about 3 minutes, or until thick and very pale. Mix in the vanilla. On low speed, add

continued on p. 38

about one-third of the dry ingredients, then add one-third of
the butter, and continue alternating the remaining flour and
butter. Add the chocolate and mix to combine. (The batter can
be refrigerated for up to 1 week.)

Spread the batter evenly in the pan. Bake for 40 to 45 minutes,
until a cake tester or wooden skewer poked into the center
comes out with just a few moist crumbs sticking to it. If the pick
comes out wet, test a second time, because you may have
hit a piece of chocolate chip; then bake for a few minutes longer
if necessary. Cool in the pan until the brownie is just a bit
warmer than room temperature.

Run a knife around the edges if not using a silicone mold, and
invert the brownie onto a cutting board. Cut into 12 rectangles.
Dust the tops with powdered sugar just before serving. (The
brownies can be stored in an airtight container for up to 2 days.)

BEST OF THE BEST EXCLUSIVE

Slow-cooking duck in a skillet renders the fat, resulting in crackly skin and moist meat. The duck here is fabulous with the mushrooms and cranberry sauce, but it's also terrific with just one accompaniment.

DUCK WITH MUSHROOMS & CRANBERRY SAUCE

SERVES 6

- 1 pound fresh cranberries
- ½ cup plus 2 tablespoons sugar
- 2 teaspoons finely grated orange zest
- 1½ teaspoons finely grated lemon zest
- ⅓ cup fresh orange juice
- 1½ teaspoons fresh lemon juice
- Pinch of ground cloves
- Pinch of freshly grated nutmeg
- Pinch of cinnamon
- Three 1-pound Moulard duck breasts
- Kosher salt and freshly ground pepper
- 1 tablespoon canola oil
- 12 ounces oyster mushrooms, tough stems discarded
- 2 tablespoons unsalted butter
- 1 medium shallot, minced
- 1 teaspoon thyme leaves, chopped
- ⅓ cup low-sodium chicken broth

EDITOR'S WINE CHOICE

Tart, earthy Oregon Pinot Noir: 2007 Benton Lane

THOMAS KELLER ONLINE

adhocrestaurant.com

 Thomas Keller

1. In a medium saucepan, combine the cranberries with the sugar, orange zest, lemon zest, orange juice, lemon juice, cloves, nutmeg and cinnamon. Bring to a boil and cook over moderate heat, stirring occasionally, until the cranberries burst, about 10 minutes. Let cool until thickened, about 1 hour.

2. Preheat the oven to 400°F. Using a sharp knife, score the duck skin in a crosshatch pattern, being careful not to cut into the meat. Season the duck with salt and pepper. In a large skillet, cook the duck skin side down over moderate heat, spooning off the fat as it is rendered, until the skin is golden and crisp, about 25 minutes.

3. Turn the duck skin side up. Transfer the skillet to the oven and roast the duck breasts for about 6 minutes for medium meat. Transfer the duck to a carving board and let rest for 5 minutes.

4. Meanwhile, in another large skillet, heat the canola oil until shimmering. Add the mushrooms and cook over moderately high heat until browned in spots, about 3 minutes. Add the butter, shallot and thyme and cook over moderate heat until the mushrooms are tender, about 5 minutes. Add the chicken broth and cook until thickened slightly, about 1 minute. Season with salt and pepper.

5. Slice the duck breasts crosswise and transfer to plates. Serve with the mushrooms and cranberry sauce.

MAKE AHEAD The cranberry sauce can be refrigerated for up to 2 weeks.

CHICKEN AND DUMPLINGS, P. 44

REAL CAJUN

Donald Link with Paula Disbrowe

Finally, here's a book on authentic Cajun cuisine, not the insanely spicy, blackened foods popularized on TV. Donald Link, the chef-owner of New Orleans restaurants Herbsaint and Cochon, explains: Cajun cuisine was forged by French exiles from Canada and Germans with butchering and sausage-making expertise who immigrated to the swamps of Acadiana on the Gulf Coast. It's rustic, often one-pot cooking. (Creole cuisine, a mix of European, African and West Indian flavors, is fancier.) Pork is crucial, and, Link insists, the food isn't necessarily spicy. His Chicken and Dumplings does contain chiles, but the dish is well seasoned, not fiery. Along with a rich Cheesy Spoonbread, it's one of the standouts in this enlightening, enticing book.

Published by Clarkson Potter, $35

Link thickens the luxurious gravy on the chicken here with a traditional Cajun roux, a mixture of flour and oil that's cooked in a skillet until it turns golden brown.

CHICKEN SAUCE PIQUANT

SERVES 4 TO 6

1½ tablespoons salt
2 teaspoons ground black pepper
½ teaspoon ground white pepper
2 teaspoons cayenne pepper
2 teaspoons chile powder
1 teaspoon paprika
One 3- to 4-pound chicken, boned and cut into 1-inch cubes
¾ cup vegetable oil or lard
1 cup all-purpose flour
1 small onion, diced
3 celery stalks, diced
1 small poblano chile, seeded and diced
1 tablespoon finely chopped garlic
5 plum tomatoes, diced
2 cups canned tomatoes
5 cups chicken broth
1 tablespoon dried thyme
4 bay leaves
4 dashes of hot sauce
Steamed rice
Thinly sliced scallions, for garnish

EDITOR'S WINE CHOICE

Juicy, cherry-rich Beaujolais: 2008 Terres Dorées Jean-Paul Brun L'Ancien

It's easy to see why this dish is a Cajun classic. One chicken will feed a lot of people when cooked this way. The word piquant basically means "spicy," but in Cajun cooking it also refers to a certain preparation that involves pan frying meat and making a roux. I've often heard Cajun food referred to as one-pot cooking and this is a perfect example. If you want to save time, buy two boneless, skinless breasts and four boneless thighs.

Whisk together the salt, peppers, chile powder, and paprika in a large bowl. Add the chicken pieces and use your hands to toss until evenly coated; set aside.

Heat the oil in a large pot or Dutch oven over medium-high heat until it begins to smoke slightly. While the oil heats, toss the chicken with flour to coat.

Shaking off the excess flour from the chicken, transfer the pieces to the hot oil and fry until golden brown on all sides. Fry the chicken in two batches so you don't overcrowd the pan—the chicken should be in one layer, and not on top of each other. Reserve the leftover flour. Use a slotted spoon to transfer the chicken to a deep plate, leaving the oil in the pan.

Add the remaining flour to the oil and cook, stirring constantly, for about 5 minutes to create a medium-brown, peanut butter–colored roux. Add the onion, celery, poblano, and garlic and cook 5 minutes more. Add the chicken, tomatoes, broth, thyme, bay leaves, and hot sauce. Simmer over low heat for 45 minutes, stirring occasionally, until thickened to a light gravy and the chicken is tender enough to shred with a fork. Taste and adjust seasonings, adding more salt or hot sauce as desired. Serve over rice, garnished with scallions.

This version of the Southern staple is just right. Everything's surprisingly light, from the gravy to the dumplings. And the combination of cayenne pepper and jalapeño adds a nice kick.

CHICKEN & DUMPLINGS

SERVES 6

DUMPLINGS

- 1 cup all-purpose flour
- 2 teaspoons baking powder
- 1 teaspoon dried oregano, crumbled
- ¼ teaspoon cayenne pepper

Scant teaspoon ground black pepper

Scant teaspoon salt

- 1 large egg
- ½ small onion, finely minced
- 2 tablespoons butter, melted
- ½ cup whole milk

CHICKEN STEW

- ½ cup all-purpose flour
- 1 whole chicken, cut into 8 serving pieces
- 1 tablespoon salt, plus more as needed
- 1 teaspoon ground black pepper, plus more as needed
- ¼ teaspoon cayenne pepper (or other pure ground chile), plus more as needed
- ¼ cup vegetable oil
- 1 small onion, chopped
- 1 celery stalk, chopped
- 1 medium carrot, chopped
- 1 jalapeño pepper, stemmed, seeded, and minced
- 3 garlic cloves, minced
- 1 tablespoon finely chopped thyme leaves
- ½ cup dry white wine
- ⅓ cup (⅔ stick) butter
- 2 quarts chicken broth
- 2 tablespoons olive oil
- 6 ounces cremini mushrooms, sliced

Over the years, I have done countless versions of this dish, and this version is the best I've made. Cooking the chicken on the bone always adds flavor that can't be beat. Making the broth from the vegetable scraps and chicken bones, and then cooking the chicken in that liquid, intensifies the flavors or, as we say in the biz, fortifies *the dish. Remember to cook this slowly, over low heat, so that the flavors have time to develop. Cooking this dish gently will also help the chicken keep its shape, yet make it amazingly tender and moist.*

I usually use cremini mushrooms in this recipe, but I've had wonderful results with wild mushrooms. Feel free to substitute pricier mushrooms like chanterelles, morels, or porcini.

Take the time to chill the dumpling batter, which helps it hold its shape in the broth. Some people sauté their onions for dumplings, but I like the raw onion taste.

To prepare the dumplings, whisk together the flour, baking powder, oregano, cayenne, black pepper, and salt in a medium bowl. In a small bowl, whisk together the egg, onion, melted butter, and milk. Using a fork, stir wet ingredients into dry ingredients just until blended; do not overmix. When you scoop up a spoonful of batter and turn the spoon on its side, the batter should fall *slowly* off the spoon; if it runs off the spoon, it's too soft and you need to add a few more tablespoons flour. You can use the batter immediately, but I prefer to chill it for at least 30 minutes.

While the dumplings chill, make the chicken stew. Place the flour in a large mixing bowl. Season the chicken pieces with the salt, pepper, and cayenne, then toss with the flour until evenly

AUTHOR'S WINE CHOICE

Go for a dry white, like an un-oaked Chardonnay or Italian Pinot Grigio. Avoid whites that are fruity because they will overpower the other flavors.

coated. Heat the vegetable oil in a large, deep skillet over medium-high heat. When the skillet is hot but not smoking, add the chicken (in batches if necessary, so you don't overcrowd the skillet). Reserve the remaining dredging flour. Cook the chicken until golden brown on all sides (using tongs to turn), 10 to 12 minutes.

Transfer the browned chicken to a plate as you continue to brown the remaining pieces. When the chicken is browned, pour out half the oil in the pan and discard. Add the onion, celery, carrot, jalapeño, garlic, and thyme to the skillet, and season generously with salt, pepper, and a pinch of cayenne. Cook, stirring, until the vegetables are tender, about 8 minutes. Add the wine, wait 20 seconds, and then add the butter and cook, stirring, until it melts, making a buttery base to receive the remaining dredging flour. Add the flour and stir until the vegetables are evenly coated. Add the chicken broth to the vegetables, stir gently, and bring to a simmer.

Heat 1 tablespoon of the olive oil in a separate medium skillet over medium-high heat. When the skillet is hot but not smoking, sauté half the mushrooms until crisp and browned, 4 to 5 minutes. Add the cooked mushrooms to the vegetable mixture and repeat the process with the remaining oil and mushrooms.

Add the chicken to the stew and simmer for about 1 hour and 15 minutes (skimming the excess fat from the top of the cooking liquid), until the chicken is fork-tender but before it is falling off the bones.

Preheat the oven to 450°F. Transfer the stew to a large ovenproof skillet or Dutch oven and return to a simmer over medium heat. Use a tablespoon to scoop ovals of the dumpling batter, using another spoon to gently scrape the batter off the first spoon, onto the stew. Transfer the skillet to the oven and bake until the dumplings are lightly golden (but not overly dry), about 20 minutes. Allow the stew to cool slightly, then serve in shallow bowls.

REAL CAJUN
Donald Link with Paula Disbrowe

A good spoonbread—the pudding-like cornmeal side dish—should be fluffy, rich and a fine partner to many different main courses. This melt-in-the-mouth version is all those things.

CHEESY SPOONBREAD

SERVES 4 TO 6 AS A SIDE DISH

- 2½ cups milk
- 1 cup white cornmeal
- Butter for greasing, plus 1 tablespoon
- 3 eggs, separated
- 1 cup grated cheddar cheese
- 1 cup chopped scallions
- 2 teaspoons salt
- ¼ teaspoon black pepper
- ¼ teaspoon cayenne pepper

AUTHOR'S NOTE

At Cochon, we serve this spoonbread alongside okra and tomatoes, but it is a really versatile side dish. It goes well with everything from roasted chicken and black-eyed peas to sautéed shrimp dishes. One really great way to serve this spoonbread is to let it cool, cut it into squares, then sauté the squares in butter until crisp. But that takes time and patience, which is why most people just grab a spoon and dig in.

Although spoonbread is a Southern staple, I did not discover it personally until later in life. What a shame—once I tasted the warm, light, and creamy dish I fell in love with it. I've heard some people refer to spoonbread as a cornbread soufflé, which is a pretty fair description. Cornbread generally makes for a good side because it absorbs the juice of what it's served with. Spoonbread does that as well, but it can be pretty luxurious on its own.

Preheat the oven to 375°F. Butter an 8-by-12-inch baking dish.

In a medium saucepan, bring the milk to a boil over medium-high heat, then whisk in the cornmeal and the tablespoon of butter, and stir until smooth. Whisk the egg yolks in a small bowl, then temper them by stirring a small amount of the hot cornmeal mixture into the eggs, and then stirring that mixture back into the pot. Stir in the cheese, scallions, salt, pepper, and cayenne until well combined, and cook for about 2 minutes, stirring. Remove from the heat and set aside.

In the bowl of an electric mixture (or by hand), beat the egg whites to stiff peaks, and then fold them into the cornmeal mixture.

Pour the spoonbread into the prepared pan and bake, uncovered, for about 40 minutes, or until the spoonbread mixture is set. (To test for doneness, insert a toothpick or chopstick into the center of the spoonbread; if it comes out mostly clean, it's done. If there is wet batter clinging to the toothpick, bake the dish another 5 to 10 minutes.)

Link uses the confit method for this decadent chicken: He submerges the legs in oil (he also likes duck fat) and bakes them until succulent, then crisps the pieces in a skillet.

CHICKEN LEG CONFIT WITH LEMON-OLIVE VINAIGRETTE

SERVES 4

- 1 tablespoon kosher salt
- 1 teaspoon ground fennel
- 1 teaspoon ground allspice
- 4 whole chicken legs (2 pounds total)
- 1 tablespoon plus ½ teaspoon thyme leaves, coarsely chopped
- 2 garlic cloves, thinly sliced
- 6 cups vegetable oil or melted lard or duck fat
- ¼ cup extra-virgin olive oil
- 1 teaspoon finely grated lemon zest
- 2 tablespoons fresh lemon juice
- 1 tablespoon sherry vinegar
- ¼ cup pitted kalamata olives, coarsely chopped
- ¼ cup pitted Spanish green olives, coarsely chopped
- Freshly ground pepper

EDITOR'S WINE CHOICE

Citrusy, medium-bodied
Italian white: 2008 Bibi Graetz
Casamatta Bianco Vermentino

DONALD LINK ONLINE
linkrestaurantgroup.com

1. In a small bowl, mix the salt with the fennel and allspice. Season the chicken legs all over and under the skin with the spice mixture. Tuck 1 tablespoon of the thyme and the sliced garlic under the chicken skin. Transfer the chicken legs to a plate, cover with plastic wrap and refrigerate overnight.

2. Preheat the oven to 275°F. Gently pat the chicken dry, being careful not to wipe off any of the spice mixture. Transfer the chicken legs to a large enameled cast-iron casserole, arranging them so they fit snugly in a single layer. Pour the vegetable oil over the chicken; the chicken should be completely submerged. Transfer the casserole to the oven and bake for 2 hours, until the chicken is tender.

3. Meanwhile, in a medium bowl, mix the olive oil with the lemon zest, lemon juice, sherry vinegar, olives and the remaining ½ teaspoon of thyme. Season the vinaigrette with pepper.

4. Increase the oven temperature to 400°F. Transfer the chicken legs to a rack set over a baking sheet and let stand until the skin has dried, about 20 minutes. Reserve the oil.

5. In a large ovenproof skillet, heat 1 tablespoon of the chicken cooking oil until shimmering. Add the chicken legs, skin side down, and cook until the skin begins to crisp, about 3 minutes. Transfer the skillet to the oven and roast for about 7 minutes, until the chicken is heated through and the skin is very crisp. Transfer the chicken to plates, spoon the vinaigrette around and serve.

MAKE AHEAD The chicken can be prepared through Step 2 and refrigerated (covered in the oil) for up to 3 days.

FLORIDA COAST
PICKLED SHRIMP,
P. 50

DOWN HOME
WITH THE NEELYS

Patrick & Gina Neely with Paula Disbrowe

Owners of Neely's Bar-B-Que in Memphis and Nashville and hosts of the cooking show *Down Home with the Neelys,* Pat and Gina Neely have written an entertaining, sizzling Southern love story. Gina: "They call me the spice fairy on our show, but my husband is the *hot man*!" Their debut cookbook is a "he said, she said" introduction to Southern home cooking and Memphis-style (sweet-and-tangy) barbecue. The Neelys love pork and add crispy bacon to mac and cheese and Pimento Cheese Melts. (There's even a pig print on the book's endpapers, and a recipe for cookies cut into piggy shapes.) All that pork is balanced by recipes like pickled shrimp and broccoli-cheddar cornbread. With two big personalities and recipes that work perfectly, this book is great fun.

Published by Alfred A. Knopf, $27.95

These fresh, festive pickled shrimp are an inventive and light hors d'oeuvre. They're also a great make-ahead dish and a fabulous hostess gift—just present them in a glass jar.

FLORIDA COAST PICKLED SHRIMP

SERVES 6 TO 8

One 3-ounce bag crab-boil spices (such as Zatarain's)
4 teaspoons kosher salt
2 lemons, quartered
2 pounds medium shrimp, shelled and deveined if you wish (see Note)
2 cups vegetable oil
1 cup red-wine vinegar
½ cup fresh lime juice
2 tablespoons Creole mustard
2 teaspoons black peppercorns
2 teaspoons fennel seeds
1 teaspoon crushed red-pepper flakes
4 garlic cloves, peeled and crushed
4 bay leaves
2 large sweet onions, thinly sliced
2 large carrots, thinly sliced
2 lemons, thinly sliced

EDITOR'S WINE CHOICE

Lively, refreshing sparkling wine:
NV Cristalino Brut Cava

Gina: We've taken a few memorable family vacations to the Gulf Coast of Florida, which is a great place to indulge our passion for the beach—and fresh shrimp.

In a large pot, combine the crab boil, 2 teaspoons of the salt, the lemon quarters, and 8 cups water. Bring the mixture to a boil, and boil for 5 minutes. Add the shrimp, and cook until they are pink and cooked through, about 3 minutes. Drain the shrimp in a colander, and discard the crab boil and lemon.

In a small saucepan, whisk together the oil, vinegar, lime juice, Creole mustard, peppercorns, fennel seeds, red-pepper flakes, garlic, bay leaves, and the remaining 2 teaspoons salt. Bring to a boil, then reduce the heat and simmer for 2 minutes. Remove the pan from the heat, stir in the onions and carrots, and cool completely. Place the shrimp in a large nonreactive mixing bowl or container (sealable plastic storage containers work great), and cover with the marinade. Toss with the lemon slices, cover tightly, and refrigerate for at least 8 hours (or for up to 2 days), tossing every 4 or so hours, before serving. To serve the pickled shrimp, use a slotted spoon to transfer the shrimp and goodies (pickled veggies, spices) to a serving bowl, then add just enough liquid to keep everything moist (using the entire bowl of pickling liquid would be too messy).

NOTE We call for the shrimp to be shelled and deveined in this recipe, because it allows them to really soak up the marinade. But if you are pressed for time, and your friends don't mind getting their nails dirty, leave the shells on. The shrimp are just as good, and the extra effort your friends have to exert may produce an unexpected benefit: leftovers!

Using crushed potato chips and crumbled bacon instead of the usual bread crumbs for this excellent mac and cheese is ingenious: The crunchy, salty topping is utterly delicious.

CHEESY CORKSCREWS WITH CRUNCHY BACON TOPPING

SERVES 6 TO 8

CHEESY CORKSCREWS

6 tablespoons butter, plus more for greasing

Kosher salt

1 pound cavatappi (or other tubular pasta)

½ cup all-purpose flour

4 cups whole milk, warmed

1 teaspoon dry mustard powder

1 teaspoon salt

¼ teaspoon freshly ground black pepper

¼ teaspoon cayenne pepper

Pinch freshly grated nutmeg

Dash hot sauce

Dash Worcestershire sauce

4 cups grated sharp white cheddar cheese

1¼ cups grated Pecorino Romano cheese

CRUNCHY BACON TOPPING

1½ cups crushed potato chips

½ cup grated Pecorino Romano cheese

5 slices cooked bacon, crumbled

3 tablespoons chopped fresh flat-leaf parsley

EDITOR'S WINE CHOICE

Smoky, rich Syrah: 2008 Charles Smith Wines Boom Boom!

Pat: When I was growing up in Memphis, everyone had their own special mac-and-cheese recipe. My girls love experimenting with different pasta, and we fell in love with cavatappi, because its tubular spiral shape holds plenty of cheese sauce, making every forkful a delight (of course, old-fashioned elbows will also work just fine). Served alongside roast chicken, or with a simple green salad and a glass of great red wine, this is the ultimate comfort food.

Heat the oven to 375°F. Butter a 3-quart casserole dish.

Bring a large pot of generously salted water to a boil, and cook the pasta until it's al dente. Melt the butter in a large saucepan over medium heat. Add the flour; cook, stirring, for 1 minute. Whisk in the warmed milk, and bring to a simmer, whisking constantly (the mixture will thicken as the heat increases).

Stir the dry mustard, salt, black pepper, cayenne, nutmeg, hot sauce, and Worcestershire sauce into the thickened milk. Stir in 3 cups of the cheddar, and the Pecorino Romano, until the cheeses melt.

Add the cooked pasta to the cheese sauce; toss to combine. Pour the cheese-apalooza mixture into the prepared casserole.

Make the topping

In a medium bowl, combine the potato chips, Pecorino Romano, crumbled bacon, parsley, and the remaining cheddar. Sprinkle the crumb mixture on top of the macaroni and cheese, and bake for 35 minutes. For a crunchier topping, finish under the broiler for 3 minutes, until golden brown and crisp. Remove from the oven, and cool for 5 minutes before serving.

This cornbread is so moist that it's almost spoonable. The base is a boxed mix, which works quite well but can be a little sweet. For a more savory version, use your favorite cornbread recipe.

BROCCOLI CHEDDAR CORNBREAD

SERVES 6

- ½ cup unsalted butter
- 1 medium onion, chopped
- 2 garlic cloves, minced
- One 10-ounce package frozen chopped broccoli, thawed but not drained (or see headnote)
- Two 8½-ounce boxes cornbread mix
- ½ cup whole milk
- One 8-ounce container cottage cheese
- 4 large eggs
- 1 tablespoon salt
- 1 cup plus 2 tablespoons grated sharp cheddar cheese, for topping

Handwritten annotations: ½ c / a little / 1 clove / 1¼ cups steamed fresh / ¼ c / 1–8 in / 4 oz / 20 oz / ½ T. / ½ c + 1 T.

Pat: Broccoli in cornbread—who knew? But sometimes you need to go to great lengths, and be very crafty, to get your kids to eat more vegetables. The result in this instance is a moist, incredibly satisfying cornbread that gets added richness from both cottage and cheddar cheese. We call for frozen broccoli, which makes this recipe easy enough to whip together in the time it takes your oven to preheat. (You can also use 2½ cups of fresh steamed broccoli.)

Preheat the oven to 375°F.

Heat the butter in a 10-inch cast-iron skillet over medium-high heat. Add the onion, and sauté until softened, 4 to 5 minutes. Add the garlic and broccoli to the skillet, and sauté for 2 minutes, until the garlic is fragrant and the broccoli has warmed through. In a medium bowl, stir together the cornbread mix, milk, cottage cheese, eggs, salt, and 1 cup of the cheddar cheese until smooth, then pour the batter into the skillet over the vegetables and stir to blend. Sprinkle the top of the batter with the remaining cheese. Bake the cornbread in the skillet for about 30 minutes, until it is lightly golden and a toothpick inserted in the center comes out clean. Cool for 5 to 10 minutes, then serve.

This is a terrific version of Southern pimento cheese, a blend of cheddar, mayo and sweet peppers that's a party staple. The crumbled bacon on top of the toasts makes them especially good.

PIMENTO CHEESE MELTS (A.K.A. SOUTHERN CROSTINI)

MAKES ABOUT 3 CUPS OF PIMENTO CHEESE, ENOUGH FOR SEVERAL BAGUETTES

- 4 strips bacon
- 8 ounces extra-sharp white cheddar, grated
- 8 ounces extra-sharp orange cheddar, grated
- One 7-ounce jar pimentos, drained and finely chopped
- ½ teaspoon black pepper
- ½ teaspoon garlic powder
- ¼ teaspoon cayenne pepper, or more to taste
- ¾ cup mayonnaise
- 1 baguette

EDITOR'S WINE CHOICE

Vibrant, citrusy Spanish white:
2008 Martín Códax Albariño

Gina: Down South, we like our "crostini," or grilled toasts, with a little soul. So we started with a rich, creamy pimento cheese that we love and gave it a little kick with the addition of some cayenne pepper. For a truly Southern spin, we added crumbled bacon (Pat and I will find a way to incorporate pork into just about any recipe).

As a finish, we slathered the cheese spread on toasted bread and sprinkled the crumbled bacon on top, then slipped the toasts under the broiler until the cheese was just melted. Good Lord, what's not to love?

These toasts are amazing with chilled white wine. Covered and chilled, the pimento-cheese spread will last up to 3 days in the refrigerator.

Cook the bacon until crisp, and transfer to a plate lined with paper towels to cool.

Combine the white and orange cheddar, pimentos, black pepper, garlic powder, cayenne pepper, and mayonnaise in the bowl of an electric mixer fitted with the paddle attachment. Stir at low speed until well blended (there will be flecks of pimento throughout). Chill for at least 2 hours to allow the flavors to develop.

Preheat the oven to 400°F.

Cut the baguette into ½-inch-thick slices. Toast them in the oven for 2 to 3 minutes on each side, until golden. Spread a generous amount of the pimento spread on each toast, and top with a crumbling of bacon. Return to the oven and bake until the cheese is melted, about 2 more minutes.

The smoked paprika in the Neelys' sweet, delicate pancakes is such a clever idea. These would be amazing with all kinds of main courses, like pork or brisket, and just as good with eggs at breakfast.

SWEET POTATO PANCAKES

MAKES 16 PANCAKES

- 1 pound sweet potatoes, peeled and coarsely grated
- ⅓ cup all-purpose flour
- 2 large eggs, lightly beaten
- 1 teaspoon smoked paprika
- ¼ teaspoon freshly ground pepper
- Kosher salt
- 5 scallions, thinly sliced
- Peanut oil, for frying
- ⅓ cup sour cream

1. In a large bowl, mix the grated sweet potatoes with the flour, eggs, smoked paprika, pepper, 1 teaspoon of kosher salt and 4 of the scallions.

2. In a large cast-iron skillet, heat ¼ cup of peanut oil until shimmering. Working in batches, spoon ¼-cup mounds of the sweet potato mixture into the skillet, pressing slightly to flatten. Fry the pancakes over moderately high heat, turning once, until golden and crisp on both sides, about 7 minutes. Drain the pancakes on a paper towel–lined baking sheet. Repeat, adding more oil to the skillet if necessary.

3. Dollop some sour cream on each pancake, sprinkle with the remaining scallion and serve.

THE NEELYS ONLINE
neelysbbq.com
f Down Home with The Neelys
t @the_neelys

ROAST CHICKEN WITH
HERB BUTTER, P. 66

NEW CLASSIC FAMILY DINNERS

Mark Peel with Martha Rose Shulman

On Monday nights at Campanile, the celebrated New American restaurant in Los Angeles, the waiters push tables together, and instead of ordering à la carte, everyone eats family-style, passing platters of chef-owner Mark Peel's comfort food. After more than 10 years of Family Dinner Night, Peel has figured out exactly what made recipes like roast chicken and tomato soup so good in the first place. Occasionally he adds a simple, smart spin to a dish, like stirring a little bit of peppermint extract into his chocolate pudding. But these are not home recipes made chef-y. They are American family favorites, perfected.

Published by John Wiley & Sons, $34.95

This yogurt vinaigrette, seasoned with cumin, is such a clever way to make an ultrasimple vegetable salad more interesting.

RADISH & CUCUMBER SALAD IN YOGURT VINAIGRETTE

MAKES 4 SERVINGS

SALAD

¾ pound thin Japanese cucumbers
Kosher salt

5 ounces radishes (about 1 bunch), trimmed and sliced paper thin on a mandoline (see Cutting Radishes on the Mandoline on p. 60)

½ small finely diced red onion (about 6 ounces), soaked in cold water for 5 minutes, drained, rinsed, and dried on paper towels

1 tablespoon minced chives, for garnish

DRESSING

½ teaspoon cumin seeds

¼ teaspoon cracked black peppercorns

⅓ cup plain yogurt
Pinch of turmeric (optional)

1 small garlic clove, halved, green shoot removed, and finely minced

1 tablespoon freshly squeezed lemon juice
Kosher salt to taste

Cucumbers and radishes are equally at home in a Mediterranean or northern European setting. This clean-tasting, bright salad has North African flavors and cooling, crisp, luscious textures. There's a nice combination here of juicy and sweet, sharp and sour. I use a mandoline to slice the radishes paper thin. You can buy simple and inexpensive plastic Japanese mandolines that are very easy to use and do the job just fine (but be very careful with your fingertips and use the finger guard!). I prefer to use Japanese cucumbers for this; they have the sweetest, most vivid flavor of any of the cucumbers available to me (Persian, hothouse, regular). If you can't find Japanese cucumbers, use Persian or the long European hothouse variety. If you can find the large, multi-colored radishes called Easter radishes at your farmers' market, they'll add even more color to the salad.

1. Cut the cucumbers in half lengthwise and scoop out the seeds (a demitasse spoon or a grapefruit spoon is a good tool for this). Lay them cut side down on your work surface and slice on the diagonal into thin half-moon–shaped slices, about 2 inches long by ⅛ inch thick. You should have about 4 cups of sliced cucumbers. Place in a bowl and toss with ¾ teaspoon kosher salt. Set aside to wilt for 10 minutes.

2. Meanwhile, make the dressing: Heat the cumin seeds with the cracked peppercorns in a small skillet over medium heat, shaking the skillet constantly so the spices will move around and toast before they burn. When the cumin smells toasty and

continued on p. 60

AUTHOR'S NOTE

Don't use your coffee mill for spices or your spice mill for coffee. Buy two; they're not expensive.

fragrant, remove both spices from the heat and transfer to a spice mill. Allow to cool for 5 minutes. Grind the spices and stir into the yogurt with the turmeric, if using. Add the garlic, lemon juice, and salt to taste. Set aside.

3. When the cucumbers have wilted, after about 10 minutes, cover them with cold water, swish them around, drain, and repeat. Taste for salt. If they still taste too salty, rinse once more and drain. Wrap in a clean kitchen towel.

4. In a large bowl, toss together the sliced cucumbers, radishes, and onion. Make sure the sliced radishes are separated. Add the dressing and toss again. Taste and adjust the seasoning. Mound on salad plates, sprinkle each portion with chives, and serve.

Cutting Radishes on the Mandoline

To avoid catching the skin and tearing the radish on the mandoline, each time you slice, turn the radish a quarter turn.

Toasting Spices

Toasting spices brings out their volatile aromas. Toast them in a dry skillet over medium heat and watch them carefully, because once they smell toasty, like popcorn, they will quickly begin to burn. Remove them from the pan immediately and allow to cool for 5 minutes before you grind them.

To give this soup its velvety texture, Peel purees the tomatoes with toasted bread cubes—such a good idea. Roasting brings out the sweetness and tang of even humble plum tomatoes.

ROASTED TOMATO SOUP

MAKES 6 TO 8 GENEROUS SERVINGS, PLUS SOME EXTRA FOR THE FREEZER

5 to 6 pounds vine-ripened tomatoes
⅔ cup extra-virgin olive oil, plus additional for drizzling
Kosher salt
Freshly ground black pepper
6 ounces country bread, preferably whole wheat or non-seeded rye, cut in 1-inch cubes, plus 6 to 8 slices of baguette, toasted, for garnish
1 large onion, coarsely chopped
2 stalks celery, with leaves, coarsely chopped
½ pound leeks (2 small or 1 large), both white and light green parts, sliced across the grain ½ inch thick and washed (see How to Clean Leeks on p. 63)
1 small red bell pepper, roughly chopped
½ dried red chile, preferably Japanese
1 head of garlic (about 3 ounces), broken into cloves and roughly chopped (no need to peel; see Author's Note on p. 63)
A handful of thyme sprigs
A handful of basil sprigs
½ small bunch fresh flat-leaf parsley

This tomato soup is comforting, thick, and creamy, though there's no cream in it. The tomatoes are roasted first, then cooked again with a base of onion, celery, leeks, and herbs. The soup is twice blended, first through a food mill and then with an immersion blender. It may sound complicated, but believe me, that final puree with the immersion blender really pulls all the flavors together and makes a superior soup. You're making a large quantity here, so your efforts will get you two batches, one for the freezer and one for tonight's dinner. Don't bother making it if all you can find are hard, pink tomatoes. Juicy heirlooms, such as Cherokees or Marvels, are best, but good Romas will work too. If you're using juicy farmers' market tomatoes, you'll need 5 pounds; if you're using Romas, which are fleshier but not as intensely flavored, use 6.

1. Preheat the oven to 450°F, with the racks adjusted to the center and the top third. If using round tomatoes, cut them in half at the equator. If using Romas, cut them in half lengthwise. Toss in a very large bowl (or in batches in a smaller one) with 6 tablespoons olive oil, 1 teaspoon salt, and ½ teaspoon freshly ground pepper. Place the tomatoes, cut side down, on one or two baking pans with 1-inch sides, however they'll fit, and pour on the juices from the bowl. Place on the middle and upper racks of the oven and roast for 45 minutes, until the skins are blistered and lightly browned and the tomatoes are soft. Remove carefully from the oven and set aside.

continued on p. 63

2. Toss the bread cubes with 1 tablespoon olive oil and spread on a baking sheet in an even layer. Place in the oven and toast for 10 to 15 minutes, until crisp.

3. Meanwhile, make the vegetable base: Heat 3 tablespoons olive oil over medium heat in a heavy soup pot or Dutch oven and add the onion, celery, leeks, fresh red pepper, dried chile, and ½ teaspoon salt. When the vegetables just begin to sizzle, turn the heat to low and cook, stirring often, for 15 to 20 minutes, until tender and lightly colored. Add the garlic and herbs and cook for another 5 minutes, stirring often.

4. Add the tomatoes, bread cubes, and 1 quart of water to the pot and bring to a simmer. Add 1½ teaspoons salt and ½ teaspoon pepper. Simmer 30 minutes, stirring from time to time so that nothing sticks to the bottom and burns.

5. Remove the soup from the heat and put through a food mill fitted with the fine blade. Return to the pot, and using an immersion blender, puree until smooth and silky. Taste and adjust the seasonings.

6. Heat through and serve, garnished with a toasted slice of baguette and a drizzle of olive oil.

How to Clean Leeks

To clean the leeks, which are almost always sandy and often caked with mud, cut away the root end. Slice the leeks crosswise and place in a bowl. Cover with cold water and swish the leek slices around in the water. Lift from the water and place in a strainer. Drain the water, rinse the bowl, and fill with water again. Return the leeks to the water, swish around one more time, and lift out into the strainer. If the water in the bowl is sandy, repeat one more time, or until there is no longer any sand. Rinse the sliced leeks with cold water and drain on paper towels.

A tiny amount of peppermint extract in this silky bittersweet chocolate pudding makes it taste just like a Girl Scout Thin Mint cookie. Chocolate purists can leave the peppermint out.

CHOCOLATE PUDDING WITH WHIPPED CREAM

MAKES 8 SERVINGS

- 4 cups whole milk
- 1 cup sugar

Pinch of salt

- ⅓ cup Dutch process cocoa powder
- ⅓ cup cornstarch
- 3 large egg yolks
- 2 ounces bittersweet chocolate (70 percent), finely chopped
- 2 tablespoons unsalted butter, cut in small pieces
- 2 teaspoons pure vanilla extract
- ¼ teaspoon peppermint extract

Whipped cream or Whipped Crème Fraîche (recipe follows) for serving

AUTHOR'S NOTE

Note how little peppermint extract is needed here. You have to use this ingredient with caution. Mint is delicious right up to the point where it turns awful.

- 3 tablespoons crème fraîche
- ½ cup heavy cream
- 2 teaspoons sugar

Lighter and less intense than pots de crème, this creamy, comforting pudding with a whisper of mint added to the chocolate is very popular at the restaurant.

1. In a large saucepan, combine the milk, ½ cup of sugar, and the salt and bring to a boil over medium heat. Remove from the heat.

2. In a small bowl, combine the remaining ½ cup of sugar, the cocoa powder, and the cornstarch. Sprinkle this slowly into the milk, whisking constantly. Return to the heat and whisk constantly until thick and bubbling. Remove from the heat, make sure the mixture isn't boiling, and one at a time, whisk in the egg yolks, then the chocolate, butter, vanilla, and peppermint extract. Whisk constantly until the chocolate has dissolved. Return to low heat and whisk constantly until the mixture thickens again, being careful that it does not boil, then immediately remove from the heat and strain into a bowl.

3. Spoon into whiskey glasses (the pudding will fill about two-thirds of the glass) and cover with plastic. If you don't want a skin to form, place the plastic directly over the pudding. Chill in the refrigerator for at least 2 hours. Top with a generous spoonful of whipped cream or whipped crème fraîche; serve.

WHIPPED CRÈME FRAÎCHE

Combine all of the ingredients in a bowl and whip to soft peaks. Refrigerate in a covered bowl until ready to use.

This is a great version of a basic roast chicken, made delicious with an herb butter rubbed under the skin. Setting the chicken on onion slices (instead of the usual rack) yields one more tasty thing to eat.

ROAST CHICKEN WITH HERB BUTTER

MAKES 4 TO 6 SERVINGS

- 1 fat garlic clove, cut in half, green shoot removed
- Kosher salt
- 4 teaspoons roughly chopped chervil
- 1 tablespoon roughly chopped tarragon
- 1 teaspoon roughly chopped thyme leaves
- 2 tablespoons roughly chopped fresh flat-leaf parsley
- ½ cup (1 stick) unsalted butter
- One 3½- to 4-pound chicken
- Freshly ground black pepper
- 1 medium onion, sliced (optional)

EDITOR'S WINE CHOICE

Spicy, cherry-scented Pinot Noir:
2006 Freestone Vineyards Fogdog

Do not succumb to the fear of fat: This is an incredibly succulent and flavorful roast chicken.

1. Preheat the oven to 450°F.

2. In a mortar and pestle, mash the garlic with ½ teaspoon salt until smooth. Add the chervil, tarragon, thyme, and parsley and mash together to a paste. Add the butter and mash together until the mixture is smooth and uniform.

3. Loosen the skin from the surface of the chicken, taking care not to tear it. You can do this by sticking your first and second fingers between the skin and the meat, starting from the breast near the neck and moving them carefully over the surface of the bird. You can also do it with a teaspoon, rounded side out.

4. Season the chicken, inside the cavity and outside, with salt and pepper. Spread the butter under the skin, concentrating on the breast and down into the legs. Truss the chicken and pat the surface dry with a paper towel.

5. If using the onion (the sliced onion acts as a rack and will infuse the chicken with more flavor), toss with ¼ teaspoon salt and ¼ teaspoon freshly ground pepper, and place in the middle of a lightly oiled baking dish. Place the chicken on top, breast side up. If not using the onion, set the chicken on a lightly oiled rack, breast side up. Place in the oven. After 15 minutes, turn the heat down to 350°F; continue to bake for 1 hour, until a thermometer registers 160°F when stuck into the thickest part of the thigh. Remove from the heat and let stand for 10 minutes; remove the string before serving. Discard the onion.

For these tiki snacks, Peel stuffs chicken livers with water chestnuts, then wraps them in bacon. They're great for parties, as they were in the '50s and '60s, because they can be assembled ahead of time.

RUMAKI

MAKES 4 SERVINGS

- ¼ cup Asian sweet plum wine
- 1 tablespoon fresh lime juice
- 2 teaspoons minced fresh ginger
- 2 teaspoons minced shallot
- ¼ teaspoon crushed red pepper
- ¼ teaspoon freshly ground black pepper
- 6 whole chicken livers (about 8 ounces), trimmed and halved
- 2 tablespoons low-sodium soy sauce
- 1 teaspoon honey

Kosher salt

- 1 tablespoon all-purpose flour
- 1 tablespoon canola oil
- 12 water chestnut slices
- 6 bacon strips, halved crosswise
- 1 scallion, thinly sliced
- 1 teaspoon toasted sesame seeds

EDITOR'S WINE CHOICE

Crisp, fruity sparkling rosé:
NV Schramsberg Mirabelle Brut

1. In a shallow bowl, mix the plum wine with the lime juice, ginger, shallot, crushed red pepper and ground black pepper. Add the chicken livers and toss to coat. Refrigerate for 1 hour.

2. In another shallow bowl, mix the soy sauce with the honey. Remove the livers from the marinade and pat dry. Season lightly with salt and dust with the flour. In a medium skillet, heat the oil until shimmering. Add the livers and cook over high heat until browned slightly but not cooked through, about 30 seconds per side; transfer to a plate. Cut each piece of liver in half horizontally. Enclose each water chestnut slice between two pieces of liver. Roll up each liver in a slice of bacon and secure the rumaki with toothpicks.

3. Add the rumaki to the soy sauce mixture and turn to coat. Let stand for 30 minutes.

4. Heat a medium skillet. Add the rumaki and cook over moderate heat, turning occasionally, until the bacon is browned and the livers are still slightly pink in the center, about 8 minutes. Transfer the rumaki to a plate, sprinkle with the scallion and sesame seeds and serve at once.

MAKE AHEAD The rumaki can be prepared through Step 2 and refrigerated for up to 1 day.

MARK PEEL ONLINE
campanilerestaurant.com
f Campanile Restaurant-
Los Angeles

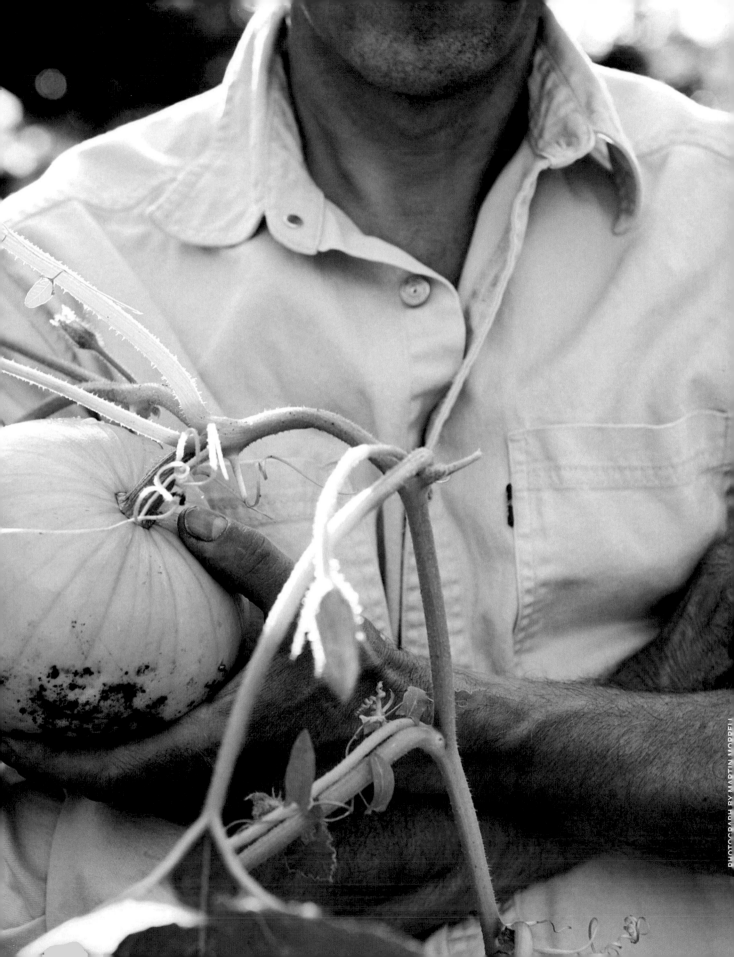

SEASONAL
&
HEALTHY

EARTH to TABLE

Jeff Crump & Bettina Schormann

In this collection of seasonal recipes, aspiring locavores are invited to follow along as chef Jeff Crump and pastry chef Bettina Schormann make their Ontario restaurant, the Ancaster Mill, more sustainable. The "earth" in the book's title is ManoRun Organic Farm, where Crump (a pioneer of Canadian Slow Food) and Schormann spent a year digging in the dirt. By chronicling their four seasons on the farm, the pair communicate their passion and depth of experience in both field and kitchen. Crump plants onions in the spring and makes French Onion Soup in the fall. Schormann sows Red Fife wheat for bread—but the first harvest is a bust. Her Blueberry Upside-Down Cake, however, made with conventional all-purpose flour, is a tremendous success.

Published by HarperCollins, $34.99

better the blueberries, the better this cake will be. Ideal for brunch, it gets a great corny flavor and coarse texture from cornmeal, while yogurt makes it supermoist.

BLUEBERRY UPSIDE-DOWN CAKE

SERVES 8

½ rec

BERRIES

1/8 ¼ cup unsalted butter

1/4 ½ cup lightly packed brown
sugar

1 1/2 3 cups fresh wild blueberries

CAKE

3/4 1½ cups all-purpose flour

3/8 ¾ cup yellow cornmeal

1/2 1 tablespoon baking powder

1/2 1 teaspoon salt

3/4 1½ cups granulated sugar

1/2 1 cup unsalted butter, softened

2 4 large eggs

1 2 teaspoons pure vanilla extract

3/8 ¾ cup plain yogurt

AUTHOR'S NOTE

Be sure the cake is still warm when you try and release it from the pan, otherwise it may stick—you can warm it up again if needed. Serve with a dollop of fresh Chantilly cream or your favorite ice cream.

Blueberries, like strawberries, have a short but sweet season. If you can wait for the tiny wild blueberries that are only available a few weeks of the year, this delicious cake will be even more special. When Chef Susur Lee visited our restaurant for an event, he enjoyed the cake so much he asked if he could put it on his own menu—what an honor.

Prepare the berries

In a 10-inch cast-iron skillet, melt butter over medium heat. Add brown sugar and cook, stirring constantly, until sugar is completely dissolved, about 8 minutes. Remove from heat and distribute blueberries over butter-sugar glaze; set aside.

Prepare the cake

Preheat oven to 350°F. In a large bowl, sift together flour, cornmeal, baking powder and salt; set aside.

In a stand mixer fitted with paddle attachment, cream sugar and butter until very light and fluffy. Add eggs, one at a time, beating after each addition. Add vanilla and mix until smooth. On low speed, mix in flour mixture. Fold in yogurt. Spread batter evenly over blueberries in skillet.

Bake until a toothpick inserted in the center of cake comes out clean, about 50 minutes. Let cool for 15 minutes, then run a knife around the inside edge of the skillet. Invert a large plate over skillet and, using oven mitts, turn skillet upside down to flip cake onto plate.

EARTH TO TABLE
Jeff Crump & Bettina Schormann

Rich, savory and deeply flavored, this is everything French onion soup is supposed to be. Instead of laying a slice of bread on top, Crump uses bread cubes, which are easier to scoop up.

FRENCH ONION SOUP

SERVES 8

- 3 tablespoons unsalted butter
- 1 tablespoon extra-virgin olive oil
- 3 pounds medium yellow onions (about 5), thinly sliced
- 1 teaspoon granulated sugar
- 1 teaspoon salt
- 1 tablespoon all-purpose flour
- 8 cups Beef Stock (recipe follows)
- 2 cups local dry red wine
- Salt and freshly cracked black pepper
- 2 cups cubed baguette, toasted
- 4½ cups shredded Gruyère cheese (about 1 pound)
- 2 teaspoons minced fresh thyme

EDITOR'S WINE CHOICE

**Earthy, juicy Pinot Noir: 2007
Goldeneye Anderson Valley**

At the restaurant we have the luxury of being able to make our soups with wonderfully thick, rich stocks. This may be difficult to achieve at home so we suggest the addition of a little flour to help with the thickening process. If there is one item our regular guests will never let us take off the menu, this is it. The recipe can easily be halved for a smaller party.

In a large, heavy pot, heat butter and oil over medium-low heat. Add onions, cover and cook, stirring occasionally, until softened and translucent, about 20 minutes. Increase heat to medium-high and add sugar and salt; sauté, scraping up any brown bits from the bottom of the pot, until onions are softened and a deep, rich brown, about 15 minutes.

Reduce heat to medium, sprinkle with flour and cook, stirring constantly, for 2 to 3 minutes. Gradually whisk in 2 cups of the stock, then add the remaining stock and wine. Season to taste with salt and pepper. Simmer for about 30 minutes to blend the flavors. Taste and adjust seasoning with salt and pepper, if necessary.

Preheat oven to 425°F. Divide baguette cubes among 8 individual ovenproof bowls. Fill bowls with onion soup and sprinkle each with a thick layer of cheese. Set bowls on a large rimmed baking sheet. Bake until cheese is browned, about 8 minutes. Garnish with thyme.

BEEF STOCK

MAKES 8 CUPS

- 4 pounds beef bones
  (necks, shanks, knuckles,
  oxtails or a mixture
  of these)
- 1 tablespoon local honey
- 2 medium yellow onions, halved
  lengthwise
- 2 bulbs garlic, halved
- 2 carrots, roughly chopped
- 2 stalks celery, roughly chopped
- 8 cups water
- 1 cup local dry red wine
- 2 tablespoons tomato paste
- 10 whole black peppercorns
- 2 dried bay leaves
- 2 whole cloves
- 2 sprigs fresh thyme

Try to get bones that still have a good quantity of meat on them. The bones add body to the stock, but the meat adds flavor. Toss the bones with a little bit of honey at the beginning to help the browning process and add more flavor.

Preheat oven to 400°F. Spread bones in a large roasting pan and toss with honey. Roast, turning occasionally, until golden and caramelized, about 1 hour. Stir in onions, garlic, carrots and celery; roast until vegetables are caramelized, about 30 minutes.

Transfer bones and vegetables to a large stockpot and add water; bring to a boil over medium-high heat. Skim off any foam. Stir in wine, tomato paste, peppercorns, bay leaves, cloves and thyme. Reduce heat and simmer, stirring occasionally, until slightly thickened, about 5 hours.

Strain stock through a cheesecloth-lined sieve into a large bowl and discard solids. Let cool to room temperature. Cover and refrigerate until fat congeals on the surface, about 8 hours; remove and discard fat.

MAKE AHEAD Transfer to airtight containers and refrigerate for up to 3 days or freeze for up to 4 months.

EARTH TO TABLE
Jeff Crump & Bettina Schormann

Peeling fingerling potatoes is time-consuming but well worth it—
they get so crisp while roasting. A little secret: The warm potatoes
soak up the creamy, tangy vinaigrette beautifully.

ROASTED POTATOES WITH HORSERADISH DRESSING

SERVES 4

- 2 pounds fingerling potatoes, peeled
- 3 tablespoons extra-virgin olive oil
- 3 tablespoons dry white wine
- 1 tablespoon fresh thyme leaves
- 1 teaspoon salt
- 2 bunches watercress (about 10 ounces), trimmed

DRESSING
- ¼ cup extra-virgin olive oil
- ¼ cup sour cream
- 2 tablespoons red wine vinegar
- 1 tablespoon freshly grated horseradish root

Salt and freshly cracked black pepper

Potatoes are something that I have planted in my garden at home. There is really something special about digging a few potatoes from the cold earth with your hands. It is almost surprising to find them under the plant. Horseradish and potatoes have a real love for one another; try some horseradish on french fries.

Preheat oven to 450°F. In a medium bowl, toss potatoes, oil, wine, thyme and salt. Spread out in a single layer on a baking sheet and bake until very tender, about 40 minutes.

Prepare the dressing

In a large bowl, whisk together oil, sour cream, vinegar and horseradish. Season to taste with salt and pepper.

Add warm potatoes to dressing and toss to coat. Divide among 4 plates and top each with a handful of watercress.

MAKE AHEAD The dressing can be covered and refrigerated for up to 5 days.

Crump's delicious variation on barbecued ribs has a distinct Asian flavor. He makes Korean-inspired pickled fennel to serve alongside, but purchased kimchi would also be great.

KOREAN-CUT RIBS WITH HONEY & SOY SAUCE

SERVES 6

¼ cup local honey
¼ cup soy sauce
2 tablespoons rice vinegar
1 tablespoon sambal oelek hot sauce
4 pounds Korean-cut short ribs
Salt and freshly cracked black pepper
1 small Thai chile pepper,
   seeded and minced

EDITOR'S WINE CHOICE

**Peppery, raspberry-scented
Zinfandel: 2008 Robert
Biale Black Chicken**

Korean-cut ribs are beef short ribs cut across the bone ¼ inch thick, 2 inches wide and 5 bones across. They are simple to prepare and finger-licking good, so if you are serving them at a barbecue party, make lots. Be a star and pretend you invented them—I won't tell. This recipe pairs well with pickled fennel.

In a bowl, combine honey, soy sauce, vinegar and sambal, mixing well. Place ribs in a large resealable bag and pour in marinade. Seal, toss to coat and refrigerate for 12 hours.

Preheat grill or barbecue to high. Remove ribs from marinade and discard marinade. Grill ribs, turning occasionally, until golden and crisp, about 3 minutes per side. Remove ribs from grill, season with salt and pepper and sprinkle with chile. Serve immediately.

These delightful loaves are fluffy and light, with a terrific crispy crust. Schormann and Crump call for wildflower honey in the dough, but any delicate-flavored honey will work well here.

HONEY WALNUT BREAD

MAKES TWO 8-INCH ROUND LOAVES

- 2 cups walnuts
- 2¾ cups bread flour, plus more for dusting
- 1½ cups whole wheat flour
- 1 tablespoon plus 1 teaspoon kosher salt
- 1 teaspoon instant yeast
- 2 cups warm water
- ½ cup wildflower honey
- ¼ cup extra-virgin olive oil, plus more for oiling the bowl

1. Preheat the oven to 350°F. Spread the walnuts on a rimmed baking sheet and toast for about 8 minutes, until fragrant. Transfer the walnuts to a work surface and let cool, then coarsely chop.

2. In a large bowl, mix the 2¾ cups of bread flour with the whole wheat flour, salt, yeast and walnuts. In another large bowl, mix the warm water with the honey and the ¼ cup of olive oil. Stir in the flour mixture; the dough will be sticky. Scrape the dough out onto a generously floured work surface and knead until smooth. Transfer the dough to a lightly oiled bowl, cover and let stand in a warm place until doubled in bulk, about 2 hours.

3. Turn the dough out onto a floured work surface and punch out all the air. Cut the dough in half and shape each half into a round. Set the rounds on a parchment paper–lined baking sheet and cover with a clean kitchen towel. Let stand until doubled in bulk, about 1½ hours.

4. Preheat the oven to 375°F. Using a razor blade or sharp knife, make a shallow gash down the center of each loaf. Bake for about 35 minutes, until the loaves have risen and browned on top. Transfer the loaves to a rack to cool slightly, about 20 minutes. Serve warm or at room temperature.

MAKE AHEAD The bread can be stored in a sturdy plastic bag for up to 3 days.

CRUMP & SCHORMANN ONLINE

earthtotable.ca

🅣 @Earth_to_Table

WINTER PASTA SALAD WITH
CHICKEN AND RADICCHIO, P. 86

HUDSON VALLEY MEDITERRANEAN

Laura Pensiero

Laura Pensiero's smart approach to healthy cooking—with an emphasis on enjoyment— reflects her background: She grew up in New York's Hudson Valley (an agricultural hub), trained as a dietitian, then went to Italy to run a restaurant. On her return, Pensiero opened Gigi Trattoria in Rhinebeck, New York, and Gigi Market, a café and farmers' market, in nearby Red Hook. With this book, her second, Pensiero serves up fantastic Italian dishes using Hudson Valley ingredients and offers a season-by-season portrait of the area. The fall chapter, for instance, features a creamy mushroom ragù along with an essay on Northwind Farms, which supplies Gigi with heirloom pork. Throughout, Pensiero illustrates the mantra she lives by: "Eat healthy, enjoy food, live well, and never sacrifice flavor."

Published by HarperCollins, $30

This salad is a fun mix of squash, apples, broccoli, beets, spinach and pumpkin seeds. The zippy herb dressing—made with light sour cream and bottled horseradish—doesn't taste low-fat at all.

HUDSON VALLEY SALAD WITH HORSERADISH DRESSING

MAKES 4 TO 6 SERVINGS

LOW-FAT HORSERADISH-CHIVE DRESSING

- ½ cup low-fat sour cream (if not available, combine reduced-fat and fat-free)
- 1½ tablespoons prepared horseradish cream sauce (available in most supermarkets; if not, combine 2 teaspoons freshly grated horseradish root with 1 teaspoon lemon juice and 1 tablespoon sour cream)
- 2 tablespoons white wine vinegar
- 1 tablespoon Dijon mustard

Salt and freshly ground black pepper

- 1 teaspoon confectioners' sugar (optional)
- 2 tablespoons chopped fresh chives

HUDSON VALLEY SALAD

- 4 medium beets (about 2 to 3 inches in diameter)
- 3 cups diced peeled butternut squash
- 1 tablespoon olive oil

Salt

- 1½ cups broccoli florets
- 12 ounces baby spinach (about 12 cups)
- 1 medium apple, peeled, cored, and diced
- 1⅓ cups whole-grain croutons (made from your favorite whole-grain bread or use your favorite brand)
- ½ cup toasted pumpkin seeds

I put this salad on the Just Salad menu as a celebration of the harvest that takes place just north of our five New York City locations. It's a simple vegetarian salad that highlights the ingredients that grow so well in the Hudson Valley. Combined with the zesty horseradish-chive dressing, it makes for a tasty and healthy meal or first course. At Just Salad, we chop all of our salads with a triple-blade mezzaluna knife. If you'd like the same chopped effect at home, use two large chef's knives, one in each hand, with all the salad ingredients except the croutons and pumpkin seeds—toss them in, along with the dressing, after chopping.

Preheat the oven to 375°F.

To prepare the horseradish-chive dressing, combine the sour cream, horseradish cream, vinegar, and Dijon mustard in a food processor and puree until smooth. Add 2 tablespoons water, or more, to thin to the desired consistency. Season with salt and pepper and sugar, if using, and stir in the chives. Store, covered and refrigerated, for up to 5 days.

Wrap the beets tightly in aluminum foil (red and gold separately) and roast them in the middle of the oven until fork-tender, 45 to 60 minutes, depending on their size. Let the beets rest in the foil for 15 minutes. Then carefully open the foil, letting any residual steam escape, and transfer the beets to a cutting board. With a small sharp knife, cut off the stems and peel the beets. Cut the beets into "rustic" bite-size pieces.

Place the butternut squash in a baking dish that is just large enough to hold it in a single layer. Drizzle with the olive oil, season with salt, and toss to combine. Roast until the squash can be easily pierced and is lightly browned, 20 to 25 minutes. Set aside to cool.

Bring 1 inch of water to a boil in a saucepan with a steamer (if you do not have a steamer, put the florets directly in the water). Add the broccoli, reduce the heat to a low boil, and cook until the broccoli is easily pierced with a fork or paring knife. Place in an ice bath to cool. Drain and set aside.

In a large bowl, combine the spinach, butternut squash, beets, broccoli, and apple. Add the dressing and toss to combine. Season with salt and pepper if necessary, stir in the croutons, and sprinkle with the toasted pumpkin seeds. Serve immediately.

Variations

Add 4 ounces of your favorite crumbled or shredded cheese, such as feta, goat cheese, Manchego, or cheddar.

Give it a protein boost with grilled shrimp, chicken, or even a few hard-boiled eggs.

Substitute your favorite dressing; this salad works well with a simple vinaigrette or more assertive flavors like sherry-shallot or even a blue cheese dressing.

Enjoy the horseradish-chive dressing as a low-fat alternative to dress other salads.

Nutrition

The vibrant colors tell all in this salad: lots of vitamins, minerals, and protective phytochemicals.

This ragù is a perfect showcase for wild mushrooms. Using a large skillet and adding the mushrooms a little at a time gives them space to brown and crisp, concentrating their flavor.

WILTBANK FARM MUSHROOM RAGÙ

MAKES 8 SERVINGS

- ¼ cup olive oil
- ½ cup chopped shallots (about 4 shallots)
- 2 garlic cloves, minced
- 2 cups chopped blue oyster mushrooms (about 6 ounces trimmed, 8 ounces untrimmed)
- 2 cups chopped orange oyster mushrooms (about 6 ounces trimmed, 8 ounces untrimmed)
- 2 cups chopped shiitake mushrooms (about 6 ounces trimmed, 8 ounces untrimmed)
- Salt and freshly ground black pepper
- ⅓ cup dry white wine
- ¾ cup heavy cream
- 1 teaspoon minced fresh rosemary
- ½ teaspoon grated lemon zest
- 1 cup grated Fontina cheese
- ⅓ cup freshly grated Grana Padano or Parmesan cheese

EDITOR'S WINE CHOICE

Earthy, minerally Chardonnay: 2008 Radio-Coteau Savoy

AUTHOR'S NOTE

I like to use whatever seasonal herbs I can snip from my garden plot. Sage can take the place of rosemary quite successfully. In the springtime I even substitute tarragon, which adds a lovely anise flavor and pairs well with the mushrooms.

We use mushrooms from Wiltbank Farm in Saugerties. Substitute the same amounts of any seasonal mushrooms.

Heat the oil in the largest skillet you have over medium heat. Add the shallots and garlic and cook until the shallots are translucent and the garlic is just starting to brown, 3 to 4 minutes. Increase the heat to medium-high and add the mushrooms, a little at a time, adding more as they cook down and start to shrink. Season with salt and pepper to taste, and keep stirring until the mushrooms begin to brown, 8 to 10 minutes. Then deglaze the skillet with the white wine, and cook until the liquid has reduced to a few glossy tablespoons, 1 to 2 minutes. Stir in the cream, rosemary, and lemon zest. Remove the skillet from the heat, mix in both cheeses, and taste again for salt and pepper. Serve immediately, or refrigerate the mushroom ragù for a few days and reheat it over a gentle flame with a touch of broth or cream.

Serving Suggestions

For crostini, bruschetta, or polenta canapé appetizers: Place a rack approximately 6 inches below the heat source and preheat the broiler. Top the crostini, bruschette, or cold sliced polenta rounds with 1 or 2 tablespoons of mushroom ragù and sprinkle with a little Parmesan cheese. Arrange on a rimmed baking sheet. Broil until the tops begin to brown in spots, 3 minutes. Watch closely so the crostini don't burn or scorch. Serve warm.

Nutrition

Mushrooms are an excellent source of selenium, a cancer-fighting powerhouse, plus lots of great minerals such as copper.

If you don't care for bitter radicchio, use milder greens such as spinach or Swiss chard in Pensiero's hearty pasta salad.

WINTER PASTA SALAD WITH CHICKEN & RADICCHIO

MAKES 6 TO 8 SERVINGS

- 8 ounces dry orecchiette or farfalle pasta
- 3 tablespoons olive oil
- 12 ounces fresh shiitake mushrooms, stems discarded, caps sliced
- Salt and freshly ground black pepper
- 1 small head radicchio, shredded
- 12 ounces boneless, skinless chicken breasts, cut into bite-size pieces
- 1 garlic clove, minced
- ¼ cup dry white wine
- 1 teaspoon Dijon mustard
- ¼ cup chicken stock or reduced-sodium broth
- ¼ cup freshly grated Grana Padano or Parmesan cheese

EDITOR'S WINE CHOICE

Fruity, light-bodied red: 2008 Marcel Lapierre Morgon

AUTHOR'S NOTE

Winter needs a little color. Radicchio adds some pizzazz, crunch, and pleasantly bitter flavor to contrast with the earthy mushrooms in this pasta salad. Prepare it with or without the chicken.

Bring a pot of salted water to a boil. Add the pasta and cook until al dente, following the package directions. Drain, and transfer to a large bowl. (The pasta can be cooked ahead of time: place it in a large bowl and drizzle with a little olive oil to keep it from sticking together.)

Heat 2 tablespoons of the oil in a large skillet over moderately high heat until it is hot but not smoking. Add the mushrooms, season with salt and pepper, and cook, tossing or stirring occasionally, until they are tender and golden brown, 5 to 7 minutes. Transfer the mushroom mixture to the pasta bowl. In the same skillet, sauté the shredded radicchio for a minute. (Don't let the radicchio cook too long; you want it to retain some crunchiness.) Add it to the pasta.

Season the chicken with salt and pepper. Heat the remaining 1 tablespoon oil in the same skillet over medium-high heat. Add the garlic; sauté until slightly browned. Add the chicken and sauté until lightly browned and cooked through, 7 to 10 minutes. Add the white wine; let it reduce to a few teaspoons. Add the mustard and cook, stirring, for 1 minute. Add the stock and simmer for a minute. Then stir in the Grana Padano. Remove the skillet from the heat and add the chicken mixture to the pasta. Toss. Serve warm, at room temperature, or cold.

Variations

Add some cooked white beans and/or a cup of peas, or substitute shrimp for the chicken.

Nutrition

Colorful radicchio is chock-full of antioxidants.

BEST OF THE BEST EXCLUSIVE

This very clever, very simple marinade relies on pureed onion, which flavors flank steak quickly. The result: tasty, tender meat.

ONION-MARINATED FLANK STEAK WITH TOMATOES

MAKES 4 SERVINGS

- 1 onion, coarsely chopped
- ½ cup water
- One 1¾-pound flank steak, halved crosswise
- Kosher salt and freshly ground pepper
- 2 large tomatoes, cut into ½-inch-thick slices
- 1 tablespoon extra-virgin olive oil
- 1 tablespoon coarsely chopped flat-leaf parsley

EDITOR'S WINE CHOICE

Concentrated, herbal, full-bodied red: 2007 Domaine Tempier Bandol Rouge

1. In a blender, combine the onion with the water and puree until smooth. In a medium glass or ceramic baking dish, pour the onion puree over the flank steak and turn to coat. Let stand at room temperature for 1 hour.

2. Light a grill or preheat a grill pan. Scrape the excess marinade off the steaks. Season with salt and pepper and grill the steaks over moderately high heat, turning once, until medium-rare, about 8 minutes total. Transfer the steaks to a work surface, cover with foil and let rest for 5 minutes.

3. Arrange the tomato slices on plates and season with salt and pepper. Drizzle with the olive oil and sprinkle with the parsley. Thinly slice the steaks against the grain, transfer to the plates and serve.

LAURA PENSIERO ONLINE
gigihudsonvalley.com
🅕 Gigi Hudson Valley
🅣 @GigiHV

SKILLET MACARONI AND CHEESE
WITH HAM AND SPINACH, P. 90

WHOLE GRAINS FOR BUSY PEOPLE

Lorna Sass

A prolific cookbook author, Lorna Sass excels at leading readers by the hand through unfamiliar territory, like using a pressure cooker or preparing vegan recipes. This really smart book (her 15th!) will help cooks feel less nervous about the strange grains that have become such a big part of healthy eating: quinoa, millet, bulgur and farro, to name a few. Sass has selected only the ones that take 30 minutes or less to cook, and she does a terrific job explaining exactly what they are, why they're great and what to do with them. Brown-rice pasta is a highlight: It's got a nutty flavor and retains its shape better than most whole-grain pastas. Sass uses it for her lush (but creamless) macaroni and cheese—one of the fastest recipes in the book.

Published by Clarkson Potter, $19.95

Most cooks have yet to discover the gluten-free brown-rice pasta sold at health-food stores and, increasingly, at grocers like Trader Joe's. It's delicious in this one-pot mac and cheese.

SKILLET MACARONI & CHEESE WITH HAM & SPINACH

SERVES 4

- 2 cups low-sodium chicken broth
- 9 ounces brown-rice elbows (3 cups)
- 5 ounces smoked ham steak, cut into ¼-inch dice (1 scant cup)
- 2¼ packed cups grated extra-sharp cheddar cheese (10 ounces)
- Salt and freshly ground black pepper
- 1 tablespoon cornstarch (optional)
- 1 package (10 ounces) prewashed fresh spinach, chopped

EDITOR'S WINE CHOICE

**Full-bodied Spanish white:
2007 Belondrade y Lurton Verdejo**

AUTHOR'S NOTE

In theory, this amount of pasta should serve five or six people, but there is something about macaroni and cheese that makes it impossible to eat only one portion, so play it safe and figure on feeding four. Then enjoy the leftovers, if there are any.

Combine the broth and 2½ cups of water in a 12-inch sauté pan or deep-sided skillet and bring to a rapid boil over high heat. Stir in the pasta and boil uncovered for 3 minutes less than the minimum directed on the package. Stir frequently to encourage even cooking. Separate any pasta that sticks together. Toward the end of cooking, the pasta will not be completely submerged.

Reduce the heat to medium-high. Stir in the ham and cheese. Add salt, if needed, and pepper to taste.

If there is an abundance of thin sauce at this point, blend the cornstarch into 1 tablespoon of water in a small bowl. Stir the cornstarch slurry into the pot.

Stir in the spinach. Continue cooking uncovered, stirring frequently, until the pasta is al dente and the sauce is creamy and thick, 1 to 3 minutes. If the sauce becomes thick before the pasta is tender, turn off the heat and cover the pot for a minute. Transfer to bowls. Grate lots of fresh pepper on each portion.

Other Ideas

Stir in ¼ teaspoon or more prepared mustard at the end.

Use half Monterey pepper Jack and half cheddar. A few minutes before the pasta is done, stir in some halved cherry tomatoes, 1 teaspoon mashed chipotle in adobo, and about ¼ cup chopped, pitted black olives. Garnish with cilantro.

Use smoked mozzarella instead of cheddar and chopped prosciutto instead of ham. Add chopped basil and ¼ cup chopped, oil-soaked, sun-dried tomatoes at the end. Garnish with grated Parmesan cheese.

This simple recipe for bulgur (precooked, dried ground wheat) delivers a lot of flavor thanks to high-quality ingredients and one small trick: including the tasty olive oil in which the tuna is packed.

BULGUR SALAD WITH TUNA, OLIVES & FETA

SERVES 4

- 3 tablespoons olive oil
- ½ teaspoon dried oregano
- ¾ teaspoon salt, plus more to taste
- 1¼ cups coarse bulgur
- 6 ounces feta cheese
- 1 can (6 ounces) tuna packed in olive oil
- 2½ cups diced, seeded cucumbers, preferably Kirby
- ½ cup pitted kalamata olives, halved
- Grated zest of 1 lemon
- ¼ cup freshly squeezed lemon juice, plus more to taste
- Freshly ground black pepper

EDITOR'S WINE CHOICE

Bold, cherry-rich rosé:
2009 Edmunds St. John
Bone-Jolly Gamay Noir

Bulgur and tuna both stand up well to the assertive flavors of a Greek salad, including feta, oregano, and kalamata olives.

Serve the salad on a bed of soft butter lettuce with some warm whole-wheat pita and hummus on the side.

Pour the olive oil into a small bowl. Crumble in the oregano and stir. Set aside.

In a heavy 2-quart Dutch oven, bring 3 cups of water and the salt to a boil. Add the bulgur. Stir once and then cover and simmer until the grains are tender, about 20 minutes. Drain. Run under cold water to cool. Drain well.

Crumble the feta with your fingers into a salad bowl. Add the tuna (including oil), cucumbers, olives, and bulgur.

Toss in the oregano–olive oil, lemon zest, and juice. Season to taste with salt and pepper and extra lemon juice, if needed.

Other Ideas

Add 1 cup cherry tomatoes, halved.

Toss in ¼ cup chopped fresh mint.

Quinoa, a grainlike South American seed containing all eight essential amino acids, is a high-protein replacement for rice in this otherwise classic paella made with chicken and strips of roasted red pepper.

QUINOA PAELLA WITH CHICKEN & CHORIZO

SERVES 4

- 1 pound boneless chicken thighs or breasts, cut into 1-inch pieces
- Salt and freshly ground black pepper
- 1 tablespoon olive oil
- 1 teaspoon smoked Spanish paprika or other paprika
- ½ teaspoon granulated garlic
- ¼ to ½ teaspoon crushed red pepper flakes, to taste
- 3½ cups low-sodium chicken broth, plus more if needed
- 1 tablespoon tomato paste
- 2 cups quinoa
- ½ cup finely chopped dry-cured chorizo
- 1 cup frozen peas
- ½ cup thin strips roasted red bell pepper, preferably fire-roasted
- 3 tablespoons chopped fresh flat-leaf parsley

EDITOR'S WINE CHOICE

Smoky, berry-scented Spanish red: 2007 Juan Gil Monastrell

I'm sure that a traditional Spanish cook would find it odd to make a paella based on quinoa, but the concept works well. More important, it tastes good.

Season the chicken with salt and pepper. In a heavy 3-quart Dutch oven, heat the oil over high heat. Brown the chicken pieces, using tongs to turn, about 2 minutes on each side. Transfer the chicken to a plate.

Turn off the heat and let the pan cool for a minute. Stir the paprika, garlic, and red pepper flakes into the hot oil in the pot.

Stir the broth into the pot, taking care to scrape up any browned bits sticking to the bottom. Blend in the tomato paste, and bring to a boil over high heat. Stir in the quinoa and chorizo. Cover and reduce the heat to medium. Cook for 12 minutes.

Add salt to taste. Stir in the chicken. Cover and cook over low heat until the quinoa is done—it should have no opaque white dot in the center—and the chicken is cooked through, 2 to 3 minutes. If the mixture seems dry and the chicken or quinoa is not thoroughly cooked, stir in a little more broth or some water, cover, and cook a few minutes longer.

Stir in the peas and roasted red pepper. Cover and let sit for 1 minute. Stir in the parsley just before serving.

Other Ideas

Use cooked chicken or turkey; skip the browning step and simply stir it in for the last few minutes of cooking.

Add 6 ounces peeled medium shrimp; stir them in for the last few minutes of cooking.

Sass has written four books championing the pressure cooker, including the best-selling *Cooking Under Pressure*. Here she uses the machine to create an excellent, creamy farro risotto in minutes.

FARRO RISOTTO WITH WINTER SQUASH & SAGE

SERVES 6

1	tablespoon extra-virgin olive oil
1	small onion, cut into ¼-inch dice
1½	cups farro (10½ ounces)
½	cup dry red wine
1	small butternut squash (about 1½ pounds)—peeled, halved, seeded and cut into ½-inch dice
3	cups low-sodium chicken broth
½	cup finely grated Parmigiano-Reggiano cheese, plus more for serving
2	teaspoons chopped sage

Kosher salt and freshly ground pepper

2	tablespoons minced flat-leaf parsley

EDITOR'S WINE CHOICE

Light-bodied, tart Italian red: 2007 Roagna Dolcetto d'Alba

AUTHOR'S NOTE

In Italian this dish would be called a *farrotto*, a risotto made with the Italian grain farro instead of rice.

1. In a 4-quart (or larger) pressure cooker, heat the olive oil. Add the onion and cook over moderate heat until softened, about 5 minutes. Add the farro and cook, stirring frequently, until lightly toasted, about 5 minutes. Stir in the red wine and cook until reduced by half, about 2 minutes. Add the butternut squash and chicken broth.

2. Lock the pressure lid in place and bring to high pressure. Cook for 7 minutes. Remove from the heat and release the pressure according to the manufacturer's directions. Remove the lid.

3. Continue to cook the farro over moderate heat, stirring frequently, until al dente, about 5 minutes. Remove from the heat. Add the ½ cup of cheese and the sage and season with salt and pepper. Spoon into bowls, sprinkle with the parsley and serve, passing more cheese at the table.

GINGERED PEAR AND
RASPBERRY PANDOWDY, P. 99

RUSTIC FRUIT DESSERTS

Cory Schreiber & Julie Richardson

One of the Pacific Northwest's best chefs (Schreiber, founder of Wildwood restaurant in Portland) and one of Portland's best bakers (Richardson, co-owner of Baker & Spice) join forces here to showcase sweetly old-fashioned recipes made with the region's stellar fruits. For confident bakers, there are tarts, galettes and double-crust pies galore. But many of the desserts are so easy they don't require even a rolling pin. To make Stone Fruit Slump, for instance, Schreiber and Richardson cook plums, nectarines and peaches in a saucepan until juicy, then top the fruit with an airy dumpling batter and steam the whole thing on the stove. There's a fruit buckle, grunt or pandowdy here for every season, and most can be made at a moment's notice.

Published by Ten Speed Press, $22

A buckle is a simple cake that's usually studded with blueberries. This rich cranberry version is sweet and nicely tangy thanks to a trio of tart ingredients: sour cream, cranberries and orange zest.

CRANBERRY BUCKLE WITH VANILLA CRUMB

BAKING TIME 45 TO 50 MINUTES
SERVES 8 TO 12

- 1 tablespoon unsalted butter, at room temperature, for pan
- 1¾ cups (8¾ ounces) all-purpose flour
- 2 teaspoons baking powder
- ½ teaspoon fine sea salt
- ½ cup (4 ounces) unsalted butter
- ¾ cup (5¼ ounces) granulated sugar
- Zest of 1 orange
- 2 eggs
- 1 tablespoon pure vanilla extract
- ½ cup (5 ounces) sour cream
- 2 cups (8 ounces) cranberries, fresh or frozen
- 1 cup Vanilla Crumb (recipe follows)

When the cranberries in this buckle bake, they split open just enough to absorb the cake batter while retaining a firm outer shell and a slightly tart bite. Half are folded into the batter and half are distributed on top with the Vanilla Crumb, creating a red-jeweled delight. This recipe is great for a holiday breakfast or brunch.

Preheat the oven to 350°F. Butter a 9-inch square baking pan.

Sift the flour, baking powder, and salt together in a bowl. Using a handheld mixer with beaters or a stand mixer with the paddle attachment, cream the butter, sugar, and orange zest together on medium-high speed for 3 to 5 minutes, until light and fluffy. Add the eggs one at a time, scraping down the sides of the bowl after each addition, then stir in the vanilla. Stir in the flour mixture in three additions alternating with the sour cream in two additions, beginning and ending with the flour mixture and scraping down the sides of the bowl occasionally. Fold in 1 cup of the cranberries.

Spread the mixture into the prepared pan. Distribute the remaining 1 cup cranberries over the cake and sprinkle the crumb topping over the cranberries.

Bake for 45 to 50 minutes, or until lightly golden and firm on top.

STORAGE Wrapped in plastic wrap, this cake will keep at room temperature for 2 to 3 days.

continued on p. 98

RUSTIC FRUIT DESSERTS
Cory Schreiber & Julie Richardson

VANILLA CRUMB

This crumb topping can be used on many recipes because it is so versatile. With a little customizing of this recipe, you can make a topping for any fruit crisp. Double or even triple the recipe and keep the extra topping in the freezer; that way, you can make a crisp on the spur of the moment.

MAKES 2 CUPS

- 1 cup (5 ounces) all-purpose flour
- ¾ cup (5¼ ounces) granulated sugar
- ¼ cup packed (1⅞ ounces) light brown sugar
- ¼ teaspoon fine sea salt
- ½ cup (4 ounces) cold unsalted butter, cut into ¼-inch cubes
- 1 tablespoon pure vanilla extract

Combine the flour, sugars, salt, and butter in the bowl of a food processor or a stand mixer with the paddle attachment. If using a food processor, pulse until the mixture is the texture of coarse crumbs. With a stand mixer, combine on low speed, also until the texture of coarse crumbs. Drizzle the vanilla over the mixture and either pulse or mix briefly to distribute the vanilla.

STORAGE Use this topping immediately, or store it in a plastic bag in the freezer for up to 3 months.

A classic pandowdy combines spiced apples with a biscuit topping. This one, with pears and raspberries, is a little more sophisticated but still irresistibly homey, especially when served right from the skillet.

GINGERED PEAR & RASPBERRY PANDOWDY

BAKING TIME 50 MINUTES
SERVES 8

- 1 tablespoon unsalted butter, at room temperature, for pan

FRUIT FILLING
- ½ cup (3½ ounces) granulated sugar
- 2 tablespoons plus 1 teaspoon cornstarch

Pinch of fine sea salt
- 4 large pears, peeled, cored, and sliced (2 pounds prepped)
- 1 tablespoon freshly squeezed lemon juice
- 1 dry pint (2 cups or 9 ounces) raspberries, fresh or frozen
- 1 tablespoon cold unsalted butter, cut into small pieces

BISCUIT
- 1¾ cups (8¾ ounces) all-purpose flour
- 3 tablespoons plus 1 tablespoon (1¾ ounces) granulated sugar
- ¾ teaspoon baking powder
- ½ teaspoon fine sea salt
- 10 tablespoons (5 ounces) cold unsalted butter, cut into small cubes
- ⅓ cup (2 ounces) chopped candied ginger
- ⅔ cup plus 1 tablespoon cold buttermilk

Position a rack in the lower third of the oven and preheat the oven to 400°F. Butter a 9-inch cast-iron skillet or 9-inch deep-dish pie pan.

To make the fruit filling, rub the sugar, cornstarch, and salt together in a large bowl, then add the pears and lemon juice; toss until evenly coated. Gently fold in the raspberries; transfer the fruit to the pan. Distribute the butter atop the fruit.

To make the biscuit, whisk the flour, 3 tablespoons of the sugar, the baking powder, and salt together in a bowl. Add the butter and toss until evenly coated. Using your fingertips or a pastry blender, cut in the butter until the size of large peas. (Alternatively, you can put the dry ingredients in a food processor and pulse to combine. Add the butter and pulse until the butter is the size of large peas, then transfer to a bowl.) Stir in the candied ginger, then pour in the ⅔ cup buttermilk and stir just until the dry ingredients are moistened. The dough will be crumbly, with large pieces of butter still visible.

Turn the dough out onto a lightly floured work surface and gently press the dough together, then press it into a 9-inch circle. Carefully place the dough atop the fruit. Brush the dough with the 1 tablespoon buttermilk, then sprinkle with the remaining 1 tablespoon sugar. Bake in the lower third of the oven for 30 minutes, then turn the oven down to 350°F and bake for an additional 20 minutes, or until the pastry is golden and the juices are bubbly and thick. Allow to cool for 30 minutes before serving.

STORAGE Covered with a tea towel, this pandowdy will keep at room temperature for up to 3 days.

For this delicate dessert, buttermilk dumplings simmer over any combination of plums, nectarines and peaches, soaking up some of the fruit juices. It's superb with a scoop of cool yogurt.

STONE FRUIT SLUMP

SERVES 8

FRUIT FILLING

4½ pounds mixed plums, nectarines, or peaches, fresh or frozen, pitted (8 to 9 cups or 3 pounds prepped)
¾ to 1 cup (5¼ to 7 ounces) granulated sugar
3 tablespoons cornstarch
½ teaspoon fine sea salt
2 tablespoons freshly squeezed lemon juice (about ½ lemon)

DUMPLINGS

1 cup (5 ounces) all-purpose flour
½ cup unsifted (2½ ounces) cake flour
2 tablespoons granulated sugar
1 teaspoon baking powder
½ teaspoon baking soda
½ teaspoon fine sea salt
½ teaspoon ground cinnamon
½ teaspoon ground cardamom
½ cup (4 ounces) cold unsalted butter, cut into ½-inch cubes
1 cup cold buttermilk

A slump is a simple steamed pudding, somewhat akin to a cobbler, that uses whatever fruit you have on hand. Unlike most of the other recipes in this book, a slump is usually cooked on the top of the stove; first you heat the fruit, then you top it with dumplings and simmer the slump to perfection. This is a perfect dessert to make on a hot day, as you will not need to turn on your oven. The amount of sugar needed in the fruit filling will vary depending on the sweetness of the fruit. It is important to choose a pot with a tight-fitting lid, so the dumplings will cook through.

To make the fruit filling, slice the fruit over a bowl so you can collect all of the juices. Slice each fruit into 10 to 12 pieces, depending on the size of the fruit, and drop the slices into the bowl. Separately, rub the sugar, cornstarch, and salt together in a small bowl, then add to the fruit and gently toss to coat. Gently stir in the lemon juice, then scrape the fruit and juices into a 10- to 12-inch nonreactive, deep skillet or a wide 5-quart saucepan or Dutch oven. Whatever pan you choose, it must have a tight-fitting lid. Let stand for 15 minutes. During this time, the fruit will release some of its juices and the sugar will begin to dissolve.

Bring the fruit mixture to a low simmer over medium-low heat. You will need to stir occasionally to prevent the juice from sticking to the bottom of the pan, but do so gently to avoid breaking down the pieces of fruit. Simmer for about 2 minutes, until slightly thickened. Remove from the heat.

continued on p. 102

To make the dumplings, whisk the flours, sugar, baking powder, baking soda, salt, cinnamon, and cardamom together in a bowl. Add the butter and toss until evenly coated. Using your fingertips or a pastry blender, cut in the butter until the size of peas. Add the buttermilk and stir just until the mixture comes together; it will be a slightly wet dough.

In 8 portions, place the dough atop the fruit, distributing the dumplings evenly over the surface. Return to the stovetop and bring to a gentle simmer over low heat. Cover with a tight-fitting lid and continue simmering for 18 to 22 minutes, or until the dumplings are puffy and cooked through to the center. Remove the cover and let cool for 15 minutes before serving.

STORAGE Sadly, slumps do not keep well. Eat this one immediately.

Kitchen Hint: Peeling a Peach

To peel or not to peel—that is the question! Most folks peel their peaches, but there is no need to peel nectarines or plums. If you want to peel ripe peaches, submerge them in boiling water for 30 seconds, then pull them out; the peel will strip right off. Instead of peeling peaches, try washing them well and then piercing them gently with a fork. Once they are sliced and baked, the peel will fall apart into the fruit and add a rosy color to any dessert.

This tribute to spring in Oregon might be the ultimate vegetable recipe. Schreiber makes a broth using five different vegetables and two herbs, strains it, then adds peas, fava beans and asparagus.

SPRING VEGETABLE SOUP WITH PASTA

SERVES 6

- 4 celery ribs, cut into 1-inch pieces
- 4 carrots, cut into 1-inch pieces
- 2 onions, halved
- 1 leek, cut into 1-inch pieces
- 1 fennel bulb, halved, cored and cut into 1-inch dice
- 3 parsley sprigs
- 2 thyme sprigs

Kosher salt

- 1 cup ditalini pasta
- 1 teaspoon extra-virgin olive oil, plus more for drizzling
- ½ pound asparagus spears, tough ends trimmed, stalks thinly sliced on the diagonal
- 1 cup fresh or frozen baby peas
- 1 cup shelled fresh fava beans or frozen shelled edamame, thawed
- 1 cup flat-leaf parsley leaves

EDITOR'S WINE CHOICE

Citrusy, grassy Grüner Veltliner: 2009 Berger

1. In a large soup pot, combine the celery, carrots, onions, leek, fennel, parsley, thyme and 1 tablespoon of salt. Add 8 cups of water and bring to a simmer. Cover and cook over low heat for 40 minutes. Strain the broth into a clean saucepan and season with salt. Discard the solids.

2. Meanwhile, in a medium pot of boiling salted water, cook the ditalini until al dente. Drain and rinse under cool water. Toss the ditalini with the 1 teaspoon of olive oil.

3. Return the vegetable broth to a simmer. Add the asparagus, peas and fava beans. Simmer over moderately low heat until the vegetables are bright green and just tender, about 2 minutes. Add the parsley and ditalini and cook until the pasta is heated through, about 1 minute. Ladle the soup into bowls, drizzle with olive oil and serve.

MAKE AHEAD The broth can be refrigerated for up to 3 days.

JULIE RICHARDSON
ONLINE

bakerandspicebakery.com

Baker & Spice Bakery

GRILLING

CAESAR SALAD BURGER, P. 112

BOBBY FLAY'S BURGERS, FRIES AND SHAKES

Bobby Flay with Stephanie Banyas & Sally Jackson

any serious chefs have opened burger bars. But few have the grilling expertise of Bobby Flay, the TV star and chef-owner of 10 restaurants. Flay is a purist: He doesn't mix anything into the certified Angus chuck at his Bobby's Burger Palaces in New York, Connecticut, New Jersey and Pennsylvania. Instead, he focuses his creativity on the toppings for his regional American and international burgers and their go-withs. This book reveals his winning combinations like a beef burger topped with "Caesar mayonnaise," romaine and Parmesan. Some of his non-burgers are genius, too: To make his Toasted Marshmallow Milkshake, for instance, he browns marshmallows, then whirls them in a blender with milk and ice cream.

Published by Clarkson Potter, $25.95

BOBBY FLAY'S BURGERS, FRIES AND SHAKES
Bobby Flay with Stephanie Banyas & Sally Jackson

The combination of meaty salmon, sweet-sticky hoisin sauce and tangy slaw here is deeply satisfying. Chopping the fish in the food processor, rather than by hand, simplifies the recipe.

SALMON BURGER WITH HOISIN BARBECUE SAUCE

SERVES 4

HOISIN BARBECUE SAUCE
- 2 tablespoons canola oil
- 2 large shallots, coarsely chopped
- 2 cloves garlic, coarsely chopped
- ½ cup hoisin sauce
- 2 tablespoons ketchup
- 2 tablespoons honey
- 2 teaspoons soy sauce
- 2 teaspoons fish sauce
- 1 tablespoon rice wine vinegar

SALMON BURGERS
- 1½ pounds fresh salmon
- 2 tablespoons canola oil
- Kosher salt and freshly ground black pepper
- 4 hamburger buns, split; toasted, if desired

SLAW
- 2 tablespoons canola oil
- ¼ cup thinly sliced pickled ginger, plus more for garnish (optional)
- 2 cloves garlic, finely chopped
- ¼ small head of red cabbage, finely shredded
- ½ medium head of napa cabbage, finely shredded
- Kosher salt and freshly ground black pepper
- ¼ cup rice wine vinegar
- 2 teaspoons toasted sesame oil
- 3 tablespoons finely chopped fresh cilantro leaves

Hoisin is a sweet yet complex Chinese condiment that you can find in the Asian section of just about every supermarket these days. The hoisin-based barbecue sauce is especially delicious with rich salmon, but it would also be great on beef or turkey burgers. The pickled ginger and cabbage slaw, which contain quintessentially Asian ingredients such as garlic, rice wine vinegar, and toasted sesame oil, are an ideal way to add some fresh crunch to the burger.

1. To make the hoisin barbecue sauce, heat the oil in a medium saucepan over medium heat. Add the shallots and garlic and cook until soft, about 2 minutes. Add the hoisin, ketchup, honey, soy sauce, fish sauce, and vinegar and cook until heated through and slightly thickened, about 10 minutes. Set aside to cool. The sauce can be made 1 day in advance, covered, and refrigerated. Bring to room temperature before using.

2. To form the burgers, cut the salmon into large pieces and then coarsely chop in a food processor. Do not overprocess. (Alternatively, you can chop it by hand with a sharp knife.) Divide the salmon into 4 equal portions (about 6 ounces each). Form each portion loosely into a ¾-inch-thick burger and make a deep depression in the center with your thumb. Place on a plate, cover with plastic wrap, and let chill in the refrigerator for at least 30 minutes before cooking.

3. Meanwhile, make the slaw. Heat the oil in a large sauté pan over high heat. Add the ginger and garlic and cook, stirring once, until soft, about 1 minute. Stir in the cabbage, season with salt and pepper, and cook, stirring once, until slightly wilted, 3 to 4 minutes. Remove from the heat and stir in the vinegar, sesame oil, and cilantro. Let sit at room temperature.

4. To cook the burgers, heat the oil in a sauté pan or griddle (nonstick or cast iron) until it begins to shimmer. Season both sides of each burger with salt and pepper. Cook the burgers until golden brown on the bottom sides, about 3 minutes. Turn over, brush with some of the hoisin barbecue sauce, and continue cooking until medium-well, about 3 minutes longer.

5. Place the burgers on the bun bottoms, drizzle some hoisin barbecue sauce over them, and top with the slaw. Garnish with pickled ginger, if desired. Cover with the burger tops and serve immediately.

This recipe is smart and easy. Flay broils marshmallows until they're a dark golden brown, then blends them right into the milkshake for an incredible caramel flavor.

TOASTED MARSHMALLOW MILKSHAKE

MAKES ONE 16-OUNCE MILKSHAKE OR TWO 8-OUNCE MILKSHAKES

Nonstick cooking spray
9 large marshmallows
¼ cup whole milk
11 ounces premium vanilla ice cream (about 1¾ packed cups)
Toasted marshmallows, for garnish (optional)

Don't laugh . . . it works, and it's good. The key is to make sure that your marshmallows are really toasted to a deep golden brown color on all sides to get the most flavor. Don't walk away from the oven because the marshmallows brown quickly.

1. Preheat the broiler. Line a rimmed baking sheet with parchment paper and spray with nonstick cooking spray.

2. Arrange the marshmallows flat on the baking sheet and place under the broiler until the tops are a deep golden brown color, about 40 seconds. Remove from the oven, carefully turn the marshmallows over, and broil until they are deep golden brown. Remove from the oven and let cool slightly.

3. Combine the marshmallows and milk in a blender and blend for 5 seconds. Add the ice cream and blend until smooth, about 10 seconds. Serve immediately.

This is Flay's clever combination of two American classics: Caesar salad and hamburgers. The creamy, crunchy salad is delicious on its own, though it's an inspired burger topping.

CAESAR SALAD BURGER

SERVES 4

CAESAR MAYONNAISE
½ cup mayonnaise
1 tablespoon Dijon mustard
2 cloves garlic, chopped
2 anchovy fillets
1 tablespoon fresh lemon juice
2 dashes Tabasco sauce
2 dashes Worcestershire sauce
¼ teaspoon freshly ground
    black pepper
2 tablespoons freshly grated
    Parmesan cheese,
    plus more for garnish

BURGERS
1½ pounds ground chuck
    (80 percent lean)
    or ground turkey (90 percent lean)
Kosher salt and freshly ground
    black pepper
1½ tablespoons canola oil
4 hamburger buns, split;
    toasted, if desired
12 romaine heart leaves
2 tablespoons freshly grated
    Parmesan cheese

EDITOR'S WINE CHOICE

**Earthy, raspberry-scented
Grenache: 2006 Torbreck
The Steading**

All of the classic components of Caesar dressing—garlic, Worcestershire sauce, anchovies (these can be your secret, but their rich saltiness is essential)—morph into a slightly spicy mayonnaise perfect for spreading all over this new way to make a meal out of Caesar salad.

1. To make the Caesar mayonnaise, combine the mayonnaise, mustard, garlic, anchovies, lemon juice, Tabasco, Worcestershire sauce, and pepper in a food processor and process until smooth. Scrape into a bowl and stir in the cheese. Cover and refrigerate for at least 30 minutes or up to 8 hours before serving to allow the flavors to meld.

2. Divide the meat into 4 equal portions (about 6 ounces each). Form each portion loosely into a ¾-inch-thick burger and make a deep depression in the center with your thumb. Season both sides of each burger with salt and pepper.

3. Heat a gas grill to high or heat coals in a charcoal grill until they glow bright orange and ash over. Brush the burgers with the oil. Grill the burgers until golden brown and slightly charred on the first side, about 3 minutes for beef and 5 minutes for turkey. Flip over the burgers. Cook beef burgers until golden brown and slightly charred on the second side, 4 minutes for medium-rare, or until cooked to desired degree of doneness. Cook turkey burgers until cooked throughout, about 5 minutes on the second side.

4. Place the burgers on the bun bottoms and spread a few tablespoons of the Caesar mayonnaise on each burger. Top with the romaine leaves and sprinkle with Parmesan and black pepper. Cover with the bun tops and serve immediately.

For this popular recipe from Mesa Grill, Flay's flagship New York City restaurant, the chef toasts bread crumbs with smoky ancho chile powder to sprinkle over roasted tomatoes.

ROASTED TOMATOES WITH ANCHO BREAD CRUMBS

SERVES 6

- ½ cup unseasoned rice vinegar
- 3 tablespoons water
- 1½ tablespoons Dijon mustard
- 2 teaspoons honey
- ½ cup packed cilantro leaves
- ¾ cup canola oil

Kosher salt and freshly ground pepper

- 4 slices of white bread, crusts removed
- 2 teaspoons ancho chile powder
- 2 teaspoons garlic powder
- 1 teaspoon onion powder
- 6 tomatoes (about 2¼ pounds), cored
- 3½ tablespoons extra-virgin olive oil

EDITOR'S NOTE
The tasty vinaigrette here—a combination of rice vinegar, honey, cilantro, mustard and oil—would be equally good on salads.

1. Preheat the oven to 375°F. In a blender, combine the rice vinegar with the water, mustard, honey and cilantro. With the blender on, drizzle in the canola oil until incorporated. Season the vinaigrette with salt and pepper.

2. In a food processor, pulse the bread until coarse crumbs form. Add the ancho chile powder, garlic powder and onion powder and season with salt and pepper; pulse until combined. Transfer the bread crumbs to a baking sheet and toast for about 10 minutes, stirring once, until light golden. Let cool.

3. In a medium baking dish, rub the tomatoes with 1 tablespoon of the olive oil and season with salt and pepper. Cover with foil and roast for about 35 minutes, until just softened. Let cool slightly, then cut in half horizontally.

4. Set the tomato halves cut side up on a baking sheet. Top with the seasoned bread crumbs and drizzle with the remaining 2½ tablespoons of olive oil. Bake for about 5 minutes, until heated through. Transfer the tomatoes to plates and drizzle with some of the vinaigrette. Pass the remaining vinaigrette at the table.

MAKE AHEAD The toasted ancho bread crumbs can be stored in an airtight container for up to 3 days.

BOBBY FLAY ONLINE
bobbyflay.com
Bobby Flay
@bflay

GREEK-STYLE LAMB KEBABS, P. 116

EMERIL AT THE GRILL

Emeril Lagasse

meril Lagasse has his name on four TV shows, 13 restaurants and 15 cookbooks. In this fun paperback, the prolific, irrepressibly enthusiastic chef tackles grilling. He shares over 150 recipes for festive dishes, including herb-marinated lamb kebabs and bacon-wrapped quail with bourbon and red pepper jelly, plus drinks, sides and desserts. Emeril is excellent at coming up with new barbecue ideas, such as his Filipino-Inspired Adobo Chicken Thighs marinated in a tangy blend of soy sauce, vinegar and garlic. And he offers useful tips throughout—for example, how to make many of the dishes on an indoor grill when the weather isn't good. Like he says, "When the grill calls, you've just gotta make it happen!"

Published by HarperCollins, $24.99

The feta spread for these kebabs is so good it could be served on its own as a dip. It's excellent with these lamb skewers, which are nicely flavored with cumin and fresh herbs.

GREEK-STYLE LAMB KEBABS

6 TO 8 SERVINGS

1½ cups finely chopped onion
1 tablespoon grated lemon zest
¼ cup freshly squeezed lemon juice
¼ cup chopped fresh parsley
¼ cup chopped fresh cilantro
3 tablespoons chopped fresh mint
2 teaspoons salt
1 teaspoon ground cumin
1 teaspoon sweet paprika
1 teaspoon freshly ground black pepper
¼ cup olive oil
2 to 2½ pounds boneless leg or shoulder of lamb, cut into 1-inch cubes (with some of the fat still attached)
8 to 10 bamboo skewers
8 pita breads, warmed, for serving
Feta Spread (recipe follows), for serving

These lamb kebabs are tasty little devils, let me tell you . . . and top them with the feta spread for something really out of this world!

1. In a large bowl, combine the onion, lemon zest, lemon juice, parsley, cilantro, mint, salt, cumin, paprika, pepper, and olive oil. Stir well. Add the lamb and toss to coat it with the marinade. Cover with plastic wrap and refrigerate for 2 to 4 hours.

2. Soak the skewers in warm water for about 1 hour before assembling the kebabs.

3. Preheat a grill to high, and lightly oil the grate.

4. Thread the lamb onto the soaked skewers, and place them on the grill. Cook, turning frequently to promote even browning, for 12 to 14 minutes.

EDITOR'S WINE CHOICE

**Ripe, cherry-scented Greek red:
2005 Palivou Nemea**

ABOUT 2 CUPS

4	ounces feta cheese, crumbled
4	ounces cream cheese, at room temperature
½	cup Greek-style yogurt
2	tablespoons minced green onion tops
1	tablespoon minced fresh mint
2	teaspoons freshly squeezed lemon juice
1½	teaspoons minced garlic
1	teaspoon olive oil
1	teaspoon finely grated lemon zest
½	teaspoon salt, or more to taste (depending on the saltiness of the feta)
⅛	teaspoon cayenne pepper

5. Wrap a pita bread around the meat on a skewer, and while holding the bread firmly around the meat, twist the skewer out of the meat. Drizzle the meat with feta spread to your liking. Repeat with the remaining pitas and skewers, and enjoy!

FETA SPREAD

Combine all the ingredients in a bowl, and stir to blend well. Cover with plastic wrap and refrigerate for at least 1 hour or up to overnight to allow the flavors to blend.

Adding goat cheese, pine nuts and fresh herbs to squash ribbons makes for a gorgeous summer side. (Opt for small, seasonal zucchini and yellow squash, which are sweeter, with fewer seeds.)

SQUASH RIBBON SALAD WITH GOAT CHEESE

8 SERVINGS

1½	pounds small zucchini
1½	pounds small yellow squash
6	tablespoons white wine vinegar or champagne vinegar
½	cup extra-virgin olive oil
¾	teaspoon salt
½	teaspoon freshly ground black pepper, or to taste
½	cup julienned fresh mint
¼	cup julienned fresh basil
2	tablespoons minced fresh chives
6	ounces fresh goat cheese, crumbled
¼	cup pine nuts, lightly toasted

EDITOR'S WINE CHOICE

Lush, citrusy white blend:
2008 Beringer Alluvium Blanc,
Knights Valley

This simple salad is a great way to use the abundance of zucchini and yellow squash that is always found in your garden and farmers' markets near summer's end. The unusual, thin-cut ribbons absorb the simple vinaigrette, and the goat cheese adds an interesting saltiness and tang. If you have one, use a French or Japanese mandoline to cut the squash—it ensures uniform cuts and makes slicing a breeze.

1. Bring a large pot of salted water to a boil. Add the zucchini and yellow squash and cook for 1½ minutes. Drain, and set aside to cool.

2. When the squash are cool enough to handle, slice them very thin lengthwise, using a mandoline or a sharp knife. Transfer the squash ribbons to a mixing bowl.

3. In a small bowl, combine the vinegar, olive oil, salt, and pepper.

4. When the squash has cooled completely, add the vinaigrette, mint, basil, and chives. Toss gently to combine. Crumble the goat cheese over the top, sprinkle with the pine nuts, and serve immediately.

The "deviled" (i.e., spicy) part of these stuffed hard-boiled eggs comes in three forms: pickled jalapeño peppers, smoky canned chipotles in adobo sauce and hot smoked paprika.

CHIPOTLE-DEVILED EGGS

24 DEVILED EGGS

- 12 hard-boiled large eggs, peeled
- ½ cup mayonnaise
- 2 tablespoons finely minced pickled jalapeños, drained
- 2 tablespoons finely chopped chipotle chile in adobo sauce
- ½ teaspoon Emeril's Southwest Essence spice blend

Pinch of salt, or more to taste

- ¼ teaspoon hot smoked paprika, such as pimentón de la Vera, for garnish

I love deviled eggs. All kinds. But the heat of the chipotle— a smoked jalapeño that is available canned—really kicks this dish up. You can find canned chipotles in adobo sauce in the international section of most grocery stores.

1. Slice the eggs in half lengthwise and carefully remove the yolks. Set the whites aside. Press the yolks through a fine-mesh sieve into a mixing bowl. Add the mayonnaise, jalapeños, chipotle in adobo, Southwest Essence, and salt to taste. Stir to blend well. Spoon the mixture into the hollowed egg whites (or, alternatively, pipe with a pastry bag). Cover and refrigerate for at least 1 hour and up to overnight.

2. Just before serving, sprinkle the paprika over the deviled eggs. (If the paprika is added too early, it will stain the eggs.)

Filipino adobo is a slow-cooked stew flavored with soy sauce, vinegar, garlic and spices. Lagasse cleverly transforms those ingredients into a sweet-salty marinade and sauce for grilled chicken.

FILIPINO-INSPIRED ADOBO CHICKEN THIGHS

ABOUT 4 SERVINGS

1¼   cups plus 1 tablespoon
      cider vinegar
½   cup plus 1 tablespoon
      soy sauce
¼   cup minced garlic
2   bay leaves
8   bone-in, skin-on chicken thighs
¼   cup honey
Olive oil, for brushing
1   teaspoon salt
½   teaspoon freshly ground
      black pepper

EDITOR'S WINE CHOICE

Rich, dark-fruited Merlot:
2007 Chateau Ste. Michelle
Indian Wells

This version of adobo chicken brings all the wonderful flavors of the classic dish right on home. You and your family will keep coming back for more! Try serving it with buttered white rice and a simple salad.

1. Combine ¼ cup of the vinegar, 3 tablespoons of the soy sauce, garlic, and bay leaves in a resealable plastic bag. Add the chicken thighs and turn to coat them evenly. Seal the bag and marinate the chicken for at least 4 hours in the refrigerator.

2. Preheat a grill to medium.

3. Combine 1 cup of the remaining vinegar, the remaining ¼ cup plus 2 tablespoons soy sauce, and the honey in a 1-quart saucepan. Bring to a boil and immediately turn down to a simmer. Continue to cook until the mixture thickens enough to coat the back of a spoon and is reduced by half, 11 to 13 minutes. Stir in the remaining 1 tablespoon vinegar. Remove from the heat and set aside to cool.

4. Remove the chicken from the bag (discard the marinade), and pat it dry with paper towels. Brush the chicken with olive oil and season it with the salt and pepper. Place the chicken on the grill and cook, turning frequently, until it is just cooked through and a thermometer inserted into the thickest part of the thigh (without touching the bone) registers 165°F, 20 to 25 minutes. Transfer the chicken to a platter, drizzle the vinegar-soy sauce over it, and serve.

EMERIL LAGASSE ONLINE

emerils.com

f Emeril Lagasse

t @Emeril

FRANCIS MALLMANN
PREPARES A WOOD GRILL
IN THE URUGUAY HILLS.

SEVEN FIRES

Francis Mallmann with Peter Kaminsky

rgentine megachef Francis Mallmann was 40 years old when he decided to abandon a career built on French technique and return to his Andean roots. In this book Mallmann focuses on seven Argentinean methods of cooking with open fire, and he proves to be a fantastic guide. One of his more intimidating recipes requires splaying a whole animal on an iron cross, and he cooks his $7\frac{1}{2}$-hour lamb in a cauldron over open flames. But Mallmann assures home cooks that preparing the lamb in a Dutch oven on the stove will accomplish the same beautiful melding of flavors. Many of his recipes are more entry-level: He simply chars carrots on a *chapa* (a cast-iron griddle) to serve with goat cheese and arugula for a great, easy side dish.

Published by Artisan, $35

This extremely slowly braised meat requires a lot of hours on the stove but not a lot of work, and the ultra-succulent meat with its rich, winey juices justifies the time commitment.

7½-HOUR LAMB MALBEC WITH ROSEMARY & LEMON

SERVES 8

- 1 boneless leg of lamb, 5 to 6 pounds (see headnote)
- Coarse salt and freshly ground black pepper
- ⅓ cup fresh rosemary leaves, minced
- 2 cups fresh flat-leaf parsley leaves, minced
- ¼ cup Lemon Confit (recipe follows), minced
- 8 garlic cloves, minced, plus 1 head garlic, skin on, cut horizontally in half
- ½ cup olive oil
- 3 carrots, peeled and cut into 4 pieces each
- 3 leeks, trimmed, quartered lengthwise, and thoroughly rinsed
- 2 onions, quartered
- 2 celery stalks, cut into 4 pieces each
- 2 small fennel bulbs, trimmed and quartered
- 2 teaspoons black peppercorns
- 2 bay leaves
- 2 bottles (750 ml) Malbec

This is one of my signature dishes, developed years ago with my longtime sous chef, German Martinegui, who is now one of the top chefs in Buenos Aires. At that time, the fashionable French chefs were slow-cooking many things for 7 hours—it was kind of shorthand for old-fashioned, deep-flavored braises and stews. Since Patagonian lamb is all grass-fed, our animals run and get exercise and, as a result, the meat can stand up to longer cooking. (We chose 7½ hours for the name because we liked the movie 9½ Weeks.) Lamb has a strong taste and it takes a powerful wine such as Malbec to complement it. If you find that the meat is beginning to fall apart after 3 or 4 hours (American lamb may take less time to become tender), take it off the flame and let it steep in its juices until it has been in the pot for the full amount of time.

This dish is best if you cook it a day or even two days ahead. Also, if you refrigerate the cooked lamb, it is easier to cut neatly into serving portions (hot meat tends to shred). Serve with mashed potatoes or creamy polenta to soak up the rich sauce.

If the lamb is not already tied, carefully trim any gristle and most of the fat from the meat. Open it out flat and sprinkle with coarse salt and pepper.

Combine the minced rosemary, parsley, lemon confit, and minced garlic in a small bowl, add ¼ cup of the olive oil, and mix thoroughly. Spread evenly over the surface of the lamb. Roll it up and tie it with butcher's string. If the lamb is already rolled and tied, use your fingers to push the herb and lemon mixture as deeply as possible into all of the seams. Pat the lamb dry, and season with salt and pepper.

Heat 2 tablespoons olive oil in a large cast-iron skillet over medium-high heat. Carefully brown the lamb on all sides, about 15 minutes. Set aside.

Heat the remaining 2 tablespoons olive oil in a *caldero* or cast-iron kettle large enough to hold the lamb and all the vegetables. Add the vegetables and brown them, about 10 minutes. Add the lamb to the pot and stir with a large spoon so that it is surrounded by the vegetables, then add the split garlic head, peppercorns, and bay leaves and pour in the red wine. The liquid should completely cover the meat; if necessary, add some water. Bring to a boil, skimming any foam that rises to the top, then reduce the heat as low as possible and cook at a bare simmer, uncovered, for 7½ hours, or until the lamb is falling-apart tender. The liquid should be just shuddering with an occasional bubble; check the meat from time to time, and turn it over if it looks dry. If your lamb is very tender after just 4½ hours or so, turn off the heat, cover the pot, and let the meat sit in the liquid for the remaining time.

Remove the lamb from the pot and strain the braising liquid through a fine-mesh strainer into a large saucepan, pushing down on the vegetables with the back of a wooden spoon. Skim off the fat. You should have about 8 cups of liquid. Bring to a boil over high heat and reduce the liquid to about 5 cups, skimming off any fat. Adjust the seasoning with salt and pepper.

Transfer the lamb to a pot, add the reduced braising liquid, and bring to a simmer. Simmer gently until the lamb is heated through.

To serve, slice the lamb and arrange on a deep platter. Spoon the juices over the meat.

LEMON CONFIT

MAKES ABOUT 2½ CUPS

4   lemons
2   bay leaves
8   black peppercorns
About 2 cups extra-virgin olive oil
½   cup dry white wine
1   teaspoon coarse salt

The combination of fruitiness, bitterness, and a floral bouquet in a lemon confit helps to focus and refine the powerful flavor of grilled meat, poultry, and fish.

Cut the lemons in half. Squeeze the juice and reserve it for another use.

Put the squeezed lemon halves in a large saucepan and add the bay leaves, peppercorns, 2 tablespoons of the olive oil, the white wine, and salt. Add enough water to completely cover the lemons and bring to a boil. Reduce the heat and cook gently over medium-low heat until the lemon peel is tender, about 25 minutes. Remove from the heat and allow to cool in the liquid.

Drain the lemons and tear the peel into rough strips about 1 inch wide. Place a strip of lemon peel skin side down on the work surface and, using a sharp paring knife, scrape away every bit of the white pith, leaving only the yellow zest. Repeat with the remaining peel.

Put the strips of lemon zest in a small container and cover completely with olive oil. The confit will keep, tightly covered in the refrigerator, for at least a week.

Charring the carrots makes them very sweet; charring the goat cheese gives it a crisp crust and melty center. Along with arugula and garlic chips, they're an exquisite combination.

BURNT CARROTS WITH GOAT CHEESE & ARUGULA

SERVES 8

- 2 tablespoons red wine vinegar
- ½ cup plus 1 to 2 tablespoons extra-virgin olive oil
- Coarse salt and freshly ground black pepper
- 8 medium carrots (about 1¼ pounds), peeled
- 1 tablespoon chopped fresh thyme
- 1 small bunch flat-leaf parsley, leaves only
- 2 bunches arugula, trimmed, washed, and dried
- 6 ounces Bûcheron or similar goat cheese, sliced ½ inch thick
- Crispy Garlic Chips (recipe follows)

Carrots are like a quiet but secretly remarkable child who doesn't attract much attention. Most often they're simply what you throw into a soup or a braised dish to "add a little sweetness." But it's because of that inner sweetness that they're so suited to charring on a chapa. *The sugar caramelizes and produces a delicious crust. They are tossed with nutty garlic chips, peppery arugula, and creamy goat cheese.*

To make the vinaigrette, pour the vinegar into a small bowl and whisk in 5 tablespoons of the extra-virgin olive oil. Season to taste with salt and pepper. Set aside.

Cut the carrots crosswise in half, then cut the halves into thick rough sticks. Toss in a bowl with 3 tablespoons of the olive oil, the thyme, and salt and pepper to taste.

Heat a *chapa* or large cast-iron skillet over high heat. Working in batches if necessary, add the carrots in a single layer and cook, without turning, until they are charred on the bottom and almost burned, 3 to 5 minutes. Turn with a spatula and cook on the other side for 2 to 3 minutes more, adjusting the heat as necessary, until they are crunchy on the outside and tender within. Transfer to a tray. Wipe out the skillet, if using, and set aside.

Combine the parsley and arugula on a large serving platter and toss lightly with half the vinaigrette. Place the carrots on top.

continued on p. 129

Reheat the *chapa* or skillet to very high heat and coat with the remaining 1 to 2 tablespoons olive oil. Immediately add the slices of goat cheese: be careful—the oil may spatter. As soon as you see the cheese blacken on the bottom, remove the slices with a thin spatula and invert onto the carrots. Toss the garlic chips over the salad and drizzle with the remaining vinaigrette.

CRISPY GARLIC CHIPS

SERVES ABOUT 4 AS A GARNISH

4 garlic cloves, as large as possible, peeled
1 cup olive oil

The French have a saying, "You must watch what you're cooking like milk on the stove," referring, of course, to the fact that milk can boil over in a flash. Case in point: Garlic chips are sweet and nutty when cooked just right, but let them go just a little too long, and they become burnt and acrid.

Using a small slicer or a mandoline, slice the garlic very thin.

Heat the olive oil in a 10-inch cast-iron skillet over medium-high heat until very hot. Line a plate with two paper towels. To test the temperature of the oil, add a slice of garlic. If it sizzles, add the rest of the garlic and cook until just crisp and light golden brown, a matter of seconds. Use a flat slotted skimmer to keep the slices from sticking together as they cook, and transfer them to the paper towels to drain the moment they turn color. (The oil can be strained and used for another batch or reserved for another use.)

The brown sugar, orange confit and fresh thyme that Mallmann pats on mild pork tenderloin give the meat a sticky, enormously flavorful crust with crisp bits of caramelized orange rind.

PORK WITH BROWN SUGAR, ORANGE CONFIT & THYME

SERVES 6

- 2 pork tenderloins, about 1 pound each
- 6 pieces Orange Confit (recipe follows), about 2 inches long, plus 2 tablespoons oil from the confit
- 2 tablespoons fresh thyme leaves
- 1 tablespoon coarse salt, or to taste
- 3 tablespoons light brown sugar

One Easter at "the Island," Peter Kaminsky and his family joined me and we cooked, fished, and read for a week. His youngest daughter, Lily, impressed me very much by how very definitive she was about things. To a parent, no doubt, that translated as "picky teenager," but to me it was a young woman with spirit— although I was vexed that she was at that stage where it was hard to persuade her to eat meat.

On the day we returned to Buenos Aires, we lunched at my restaurant. Peter ordered this pork with burnt sugar, orange confit, and thyme. To my surprise, Lily requested some and positively devoured it. There's no greater compliment that can be paid to an Argentine chef than converting a non-meat-eater.

Lay the pork tenderloins on a work surface. Tear the orange confit into ½-inch pieces and scatter over the top of the meat. Sprinkle with the thyme and half the salt, then sprinkle the brown sugar on top and pat it down firmly with your hand. Drizzle with the oil from the orange confit.

Heat a *chapa* or a large square or rectangular cast-iron griddle over medium heat until a drop of water sizzles on the surface. Using a wide spatula, lift each pork tenderloin and invert it, sugar side down, onto the hot surface. Cook them, without

continued on p. 132

EDITOR'S WINE CHOICE

**Ripe, berry-rich Rhône-style blend:
2008 Hewitson Miss Harry**

moving, for 5 minutes. If the sugar begins to smell unpleasantly burned, adjust the heat by moving the griddle and/or lowering the flame. When the sugar side is well browned, turn the tenderloins and cook, turning to sear on all sides, for 10 to 15 minutes more, or until done to taste. The internal temperature should be 135°F for a rosy pink.

Transfer the meat to a carving board and allow to rest, tented loosely with foil, for 10 minutes before slicing. Season to taste with the remaining salt and serve.

ORANGE CONFIT

MAKES ABOUT 3 CUPS

4	oranges
3	bay leaves
12	black peppercorns
About 2¼ cups extra-virgin olive oil
¾	cup dry white wine
2	teaspoons coarse salt

Cut the oranges in half. Squeeze the juice and reserve it for another use.

Put the squeezed orange halves in a large saucepan and add the bay leaves, peppercorns, 3 tablespoons of the olive oil, the white wine, and salt. Add enough water to completely cover the oranges and bring to a boil. Reduce the heat and cook until the orange peel is tender, about 25 minutes. Remove from the heat and allow to cool in the liquid.

Drain the oranges and tear the peel into rough strips about 1 inch wide. Place a strip of orange peel skin side down on the work surface and, using a very sharp paring knife, scrape away every bit of the white pith, leaving only the orange zest. Repeat with the remaining peel.

Put the strips of orange zest in a small container and cover completely with olive oil. The confit will keep, tightly covered in the refrigerator, for at least a week.

Mallmann equates eating this salad to "making love to summer." He combines burrata, a superlush Italian cheese, with his signature "burnt" fruit—in this case, figs.

BURNT SUMMER FIGS WITH BURRATA & ARUGULA

SERVES 4

- 4 ounces baby arugula
- ¾ pound burrata, loosely torn into 2-inch pieces
- ¾ cup marcona almonds
- 8 fresh figs, stemmed and halved
- 2 tablespoons sugar
- 2 tablespoons extra-virgin olive oil
- 1 tablespoon fresh lemon juice

Sea salt and freshly ground pepper

EDITOR'S WINE CHOICE

Bright, juicy sparkling red:
2009 Lini 910 Labrusca
Lambrusco Rosso

1. Arrange the arugula on a large serving platter. Top with the burrata and sprinkle with the almonds.

2. Heat a large cast-iron skillet until very hot. Sprinkle the cut sides of the figs with the sugar. Place the figs cut side down in the skillet and cook undisturbed until the sugar starts to smoke and turn dark brown, about 2 minutes. Arrange the figs on the salad, drizzle with the olive oil and lemon juice and season with salt and pepper. Serve at once.

FRANCIS MALLMANN ONLINE

f Francis Mallmann

t @Francisjmallman

MARINATED SKIRT
STEAK WITH GARLIC
AND CILANTRO, P. 138

SERIOUS BARBECUE

Adam Perry Lang with JJ Goode & Amy Vogler

or Adam Perry Lang, the classically trained chef who owns Daisy May's BBQ USA in New York City, barbecue means slow-smoking *and* grilling. Meat geeks can go as deep as they want into both here: Perry Lang covers hard-core techniques like injecting brine (the "serious" part of the book's title), but he has plenty of tips for weekend grillers, too. In a chapter on basics, he debunks myths like the need to bring meat to room temperature before grilling. Using meat right out of the fridge means that his Marinated Skirt Steak with Garlic and Cilantro will remain rosy at the center even while it develops a good char. Perry Lang's know-how makes the book an invaluable resource. "I didn't just want to offer recipes," he writes. "My goal was to create instinct."

Published by Hyperion, $35

Using beer to cook bratwurst (the German sausage made with pork, beef and sometimes veal) isn't uncommon, but infusing the beer with onion, garlic, caraway, herbs and crushed red pepper is.

BEER & CARAWAY BRAISED BRATWURST

SERVES 6 TO 12

BEER BATH

- 24 ounces beer (not light) or lager
- 1 large sweet white onion, thinly sliced
- 12 unpeeled garlic cloves, crushed
- ¼ cup canola or vegetable oil
- 1 tablespoon caraway seeds, crushed with a rolling pin or heavy-bottomed pan
- 4 flat-leaf parsley sprigs
- 4 thyme sprigs
- 1½ teaspoons crushed hot red pepper flakes (optional)

- 12 uncooked bratwurst
- ¼ to ½ cup canola or vegetable oil
- 12 soft rolls
- 2 batches Grilled Sweet Onions (recipe follows)

About 5 cups sauerkraut

Mustard of choice

EDITOR'S BEER CHOICE

Crisp, floral IPA:

Bell's Two Hearted Ale

It's game day. You're almost finished smoking six racks of ribs, but suddenly your small party has become a blowout. Instead of stressing, look to this perfectly porky sausage to fill out your meal. Stuffed in a soft bun, it's the ultimate hand-held, no-fuss food. Because I always end up hanging out and eating all day, I grill the brats, and then let them wallow in a bath of beer spiked with onions and garlic, so they stay moist and get all yeasty and delicious. Extras like mustard, sauerkraut, or caramelized onions certainly don't hurt.

1. Position two heavy-duty aluminum foil–wrapped firebricks about 4 inches apart on one area of a well-oiled charcoal or gas grill, and preheat all areas to high.

2. Combine the beer bath ingredients in a baking dish or disposable aluminum pan, preferably a 13½-by-9⅝-by-2¾-inch lasagna pan. Place the uncovered dish on the bricks, close the lid, and preheat until hot, about 45 minutes.

3. Add the bratwurst to the bath. It's OK if the bratwurst touch and are not completely submerged in the bath. Close the lid and cook for 20 minutes, flipping the bratwurst once halfway through the cooking.

4. Meanwhile, pour a film of canola oil into a baking dish or disposable pan.

5. Remove the bratwurst from the bath, roll in the oil to lightly coat, and place evenly across the grate with about an inch between each. Turn to brown and caramelize deeply on all sides, about 2 minutes per side.

6. The brats can be served at this point, or held in the beer bath over very low heat with the lid closed for up to 1 hour. Occasionally test the heat of the bath. The bath should remain warm, 140°F, but should not boil. Serve the brats on soft rolls, topped with onions and/or sauerkraut, and mustard.

GRILLED SWEET ONIONS

I often have a ton of these sizzling next to whatever meats I have on the grill—especially if I'm cooking burgers, because to me, caramelized onions are as essential as ketchup. With a cast-iron griddle, you can give the onions some bonus caramelization. I didn't think it was possible either, but yes, this improves on perfection.

MAKES ABOUT 2 CUPS

3 to 4 sweet white onions, peeled
3   tablespoons extra-virgin olive oil
1   tablespoon fresh thyme leaves
1   tablespoon granulated sugar
1   teaspoon kosher salt
1   teaspoon finely ground
    fresh black pepper
2   tablespoons (1 ounce)
    unsalted butter
6   garlic cloves, peeled, and
    grated on a Microplane grater
2   tablespoons red wine vinegar

1. Cut the onions through the root end and lay, cut side down, on the work surface. Cut across each half, following the natural lines, to make perfectly even ⅛-inch slices. You will need 6 cups.

2. Place a cast-iron griddle on a well-oiled charcoal or gas grill. Preheat all areas to high.

3. Toss the onions with 2 tablespoons of the olive oil, thyme, sugar, salt, and pepper.

4. Pour the remaining 1 tablespoon of the oil on the griddle and let heat for about 1 minute. Spread the onions on the griddle and decrease the heat to medium. Close the lid and cook the onions, without stirring, for 10 minutes.

5. Move the onions to one side of the griddle. Melt the butter on the cleared space, add the garlic, and stir to coat in the butter. Cook until fragrant, about 1 minute. Stir the onions and garlic together and cook with the lid open until the onions are completely tender, about 3 minutes. Pour the vinegar right onto the griddle and mix it into the onions.

6. Serve directly from the grill or transfer to a bowl.

SERIOUS BARBECUE
Adam Perry Lang with JJ Goode & Amy Vogler

Butter mixed with hot pepper, garlic and herbs transforms the steak here, soaking into the cooked meat to make it that much more delicious and melting into the juices that pool on the plate.

MARINATED SKIRT STEAK WITH GARLIC & CILANTRO

SERVES 6 TO 8

MARINADE

- 1 tablespoon crushed hot red pepper flakes
- 2 tablespoons boiling water
- 1 cup freshly squeezed orange juice
- ½ cup freshly squeezed lime juice
- 2 tablespoons honey
- 1 tablespoon Japanese soy sauce
- ½ cup coarsely chopped sweet white onion
- 10 garlic cloves, peeled, halved, germ removed, and grated on a Microplane grater
- 1 tablespoon kosher salt
- 1 teaspoon ground cumin
- 1 teaspoon dried oregano, preferably Mexican

- 4 skirt steaks, about 1½ pounds each

SEASONING BLEND

- 2 tablespoons mild chile powder, preferably Chimayo, Ancho or Hatch
- 1 tablespoon garlic salt
- 1 tablespoon lemon pepper
- 1 tablespoon coarsely ground fresh black pepper

continued on p. 140

Skirt steak has a deep, beefy flavor that can stand up to bold spices. So I take this inexpensive, easy-to-find cut and hit it with lots of garlic and a little honey to rev up the caramelization. The result is so outrageously good that it'll tempt you to take skirt steak outside of its standard role as fajita-filler. It's a really thin cut, so it should be served right after it's cooked. Have everything else ready before you throw it on the grill.

1. Place the pepper flakes in a small bowl and pour the boiling water over them. Let sit for 1 to 2 minutes to rehydrate the flakes. Combine all of the remaining marinade ingredients in a blender, or in a bowl using an immersion/stick blender. Stir in the pepper flakes and the soaking water.

Place the skirt steaks in one extra-large resealable plastic bag (or divide between two large bags). Pour over the marinade, squeeze out any excess air from the bag, and close. Roll the bag to evenly coat all of the meat in the marinade. Refrigerate for at least 1 hour and up to 3.

2. Preheat all grates of a well-oiled charcoal or gas grill to high.

3. Combine all of the seasoning blend ingredients.

continued on p. 140

CHEF ADAM PERRY LANG
AT THE GRILL.

RESTING BUTTER

- 8 tablespoons (4 ounces) unsalted butter
- ¼ cup finely chopped flat-leaf parsley or cilantro
- 1 tablespoon freshly squeezed lemon juice
- 1 tablespoon Worcestershire sauce
- 4 garlic cloves, peeled, halved, germ removed, and grated on a Microplane grater
- 1 teaspoon crushed hot red pepper flakes

About ¼ cup canola or vegetable oil

- ½ cup cilantro leaves

EDITOR'S WINE CHOICE

Concentrated, brambly Syrah: 2007 Copain Tous Ensemble

In a small saucepan, combine all of the resting butter ingredients, stirring to combine as the butter melts. Pour into a baking dish or disposable aluminum pan, preferably a 13½-by-9⅝-by-2¾-inch lasagna pan.

4. Remove the steaks from the bag and lightly pat dry with paper towels.

Season the steaks with the seasoning blend.

Using your hands or a brush, evenly, but lightly, coat the steaks with canola oil.

5. If you have a grill press(es) or a fire brick(s) wrapped in heavy-duty aluminum foil, it is ideal to keep on hand to keep the meat from lifting up and also to maximize the caramelization.

Place the steaks on the grill, keep the lid open, and do not move the steaks until they are well marked and lightly charred, about 2 minutes. Flip the steaks, keep the lid open, and repeat on the second side, grilling for 2 minutes.

Place the steaks into the pan of resting butter, dredging to thoroughly coat both sides in the butter.

6. Clean and re-oil the grill grates.

7. Letting any excess butter run off into the pan, place the steaks back on the grill, close the lid, and do not move them until they reach the desired doneness. Cook about 2 minutes for rare, about 3 minutes for medium, and about 4 for well-done.

8. Remove from the grill and place in the butter, turning to coat, and let rest for at least 5 minutes or up to 15.

9. Drizzle some of the butter on a cutting board, top with the steaks, and cut against the grain, on the diagonal, into ¼-inch slices. Sprinkle the cilantro leaves over the top.

Perry Lang gives these steaks a triple whammy of flavor: First he marinates them in a spicy oil, then he uses a bundle of fresh rosemary and thyme sprigs to brush them with garlic-shallot butter.

MARINATED TENDERLOIN WITH SMOKED PAPRIKA

SERVES 8

FLAVORING OIL

- 1 tablespoon crushed hot red pepper flakes
- 1 tablespoon boiling water
- 1 cup extra-virgin olive oil
- 20 garlic cloves, peeled, halved, germ removed, and thinly sliced
- 2 rosemary sprigs
- 2 thyme sprigs

- 8 tenderloin filets mignons, 7 to 8 ounces each

- ½ recipe Compound Butter (recipe follows), softened at room temperature
- 1 tablespoon pimentón or other smoked paprika

Kosher salt
Finely ground fresh black pepper
- ½ bunch rosemary and ½ bunch thyme, tied in an herb bundle

AUTHOR'S NOTE

Unlike the whole tenderloin, the tenderloin filets can be easily cooked to various degrees of doneness, which is a blessing when you're cooking for a group with different preferences.

When I'm craving the lushness of a perfect rosy-rare center, I grill the whole tenderloin and carve it up. But when I'm after deep, dark char and gleaming grill marks, I head straight for individual filets mignons. As if they don't get enough flavor from my herb-infused oil, I hit them with compound butter to boost caramelization. And, as I love to do, toward the end of cooking I take a bundle of rosemary and thyme and use it to brush butter on each filet. It's a way to add an extra blast of herby perfume without the risk of burning the greenery.

1. Place the pepper flakes in a small bowl and pour the boiling water over them. Let sit for 1 to 2 minutes to rehydrate the flakes. Combine all of the flavoring oil ingredients including the pepper flakes and the soaking water in a blender, or in a bowl using an immersion/stick blender.

Place the filets in an extra-large resealable plastic bag (or divide between two), pour over the flavoring oil, squeeze out the excess air from the bag, and close. Refrigerate for at least 2 hours, but preferably up to 24.

continued on p. 142

SERIOUS BARBECUE
Adam Perry Lang with JJ Goode & Amy Vogler

2. Preheat all grates of a well-oiled charcoal or gas grill to high.

3. Combine the compound butter with the paprika.

4. Remove the steaks from the bag, letting any excess marinade run off into the bag. Lightly pat dry with paper towels.

Generously season all steaks on both sides with salt and pepper.

5. It is preferable that the steaks be moved to a clean area of the grate every time they are flipped. Depending on the grill size, they may need to be cooked in batches to ensure there is a clean portion of the grill to flip to.

Place the steaks on the grate and decrease the heat to medium. Keep the lid open, and do not move the steaks until they are well marked and have a light char, about 2 minutes. Flip, keep the lid open, and repeat on the second side, grilling for 2 minutes.

Flip the steaks again and continue to cook, with the lid open (flipping, jockeying, and stacking as needed), brushing with butter, using the herb bundle about every minute, until you reach the desired doneness.

Cook about 2 minutes per side for rare, about 3 minutes per side for medium rare, about 4 minutes per side for medium, about 5 minutes per side for medium well, and about 6 minutes per side for well-done.

6. Using the herb bundle, brush butter onto a cutting board, remove the steaks from the heat, and place on top. Brush each steak with additional butter and season with salt and pepper. Let rest for 5 minutes before serving.

COMPOUND BUTTER

MAKES ABOUT 1 POUND

- 1 pound (4 sticks) unsalted butter, softened at room temperature
- ¼ cup finely chopped flat-leaf parsley
- 2 tablespoons finely chopped shallots
- 1 garlic clove, peeled, halved, germ removed, and grated on a Microplane grater

Zest of 1 lemon, grated on a Microplane grater

- 2 teaspoons finely ground fresh black pepper
- 2 teaspoons kosher salt

If you've read my recipes, you'll notice that I have a thing for compound butter. That's because it's a killer way of adding color and flavor. It's unbelievably easy to make, it's great to prepare ahead, and it stands up well to freezing (you can even use it right out of the freezer). I brush it on meats as they cook, sometimes using a bundle of herbs, and spread it on my cutting board when I'm slicing meat that comes off the grill, so that some hangs on to each slice.

Combine all of the ingredients in a medium bowl, pressing down on the butter slightly to smooth and to evenly incorporate the other ingredients.

Lay out a piece of plastic wrap about 18 inches long. Place the butter in the center of the plastic and spread into a rough log shape that is about 1½ inches in diameter. Fold up the plastic from the edge closest to you and use it as a guide to roll the plastic into a smooth log.

Wrap the log tightly in the plastic wrap, twisting the ends to compact the log slightly. Wrap in a second sheet of plastic wrap, if necessary. Tightly wrapped, the butter can be refrigerated for 1 week, or frozen for up to 1 month.

ADAM PERRY LANG ONLINE
adamperrylang.com

LATIN * TAPAS

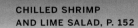
CHILLED SHRIMP
AND LIME SALAD, P. 152

SIMPLY MEXICAN

Lourdes Castro

At the Culinary Academy in Miami's Biltmore Hotel, students ask cooking teacher Lourdes Castro two things over and over: how to use a knife properly and how to make authentic Mexican food. In this book, her first, Castro focuses on everyday Mexican dishes. Each recipe is like a mini lesson because of Castro's copious notes on techniques and ingredients. To explain the difference between baby back ribs and spareribs, for instance, Castro states that spareribs are less meaty, fattier and more flavorful. But she reassures the reader that either type is succulent in her recipe for slow-cooked, chile-smothered pork ribs. By providing so much guidance, Castro makes every recipe seem easy.

Published by Ten Speed Press, $24.95

These seriously spicy ribs are seriously tender because they roast in a steam-filled oven: Castro wraps them in plastic and foil, then sets them right on the oven rack to cook slowly over a water-filled pan.

CHILE-SMOTHERED SPARERIBS

SERVES 4

- 2 racks (about 5 pounds total) baby back ribs or spareribs (see Author's Note below)
- ½ cup olive oil
- 4 canned chipotle chiles
- 2 teaspoons ground cumin
- 2 tablespoons dried oregano
- 4 cloves garlic
- 2 teaspoons salt, plus more to taste
- 1 teaspoon black pepper, plus more to taste
- 1 cup honey
- ½ cup adobo sauce from canned chipotles

AUTHOR'S NOTE

Ribs can come from either the underbelly or the back (loin section) of the pig. Spareribs come from the underbelly, and have less meat, more fat, and more flavor than baby back ribs, which come from the loin section. St. Louis–style ribs are trimmed spareribs. Feel free to use whichever cut you prefer.

It is said that ribs should be cooked low and slow, and this recipe does just that. Cumin, oregano, and chipotle chiles slowly infuse into the meat of these ribs for 3 hours before they are glazed with honey and adobo. A winning combination!

Prepare the ribs

Preheat the oven to 275°F. Position one oven rack on the bottom and the second one in the center of the oven.

Before getting started, make sure the bottom (the bony side) of the ribs are lightly scored (have small gashes). If they are not, create shallow 1-inch-long gashes throughout the bottom side of the rib racks. (This is to help the ribs cook evenly.)

Marinate the ribs

Combine the olive oil, chipotle chiles, cumin, oregano, garlic, 2 teaspoons salt, and 1 teaspoon black pepper in a food processor or blender and process until you have a coarse puree. You may need to scrape down the side of the blender jar or processor bowl a few times.

Place a piece of plastic wrap that is a bit longer than the length of the ribs on your counter and put one of the rib racks in its center. Pour half of the marinade over the ribs and coat both sides well. Wrap the plastic securely around the rib rack.

Next, wrap a large piece of aluminum foil around the plastic-lined rib rack, making sure to cover all the plastic, and seal it well. Repeat the same procedure with the second rack.

Allow to marinate in the refrigerator for at least 1 hour, or up to 24 hours.

AUTHOR'S NOTE

Wrapping the racks first in plastic and then in aluminum foil helps to maximize the flavor and texture of the ribs by keeping the marinade in close contact with the meat. The foil layer is there to keep the plastic wrap from melting. Because the oven is set at a low temperature and there is steam being produced in it, there is no danger of the plastic wrap melting. However, do not attempt this technique with a higher oven temperature.

Roast

Fill a large roasting pan with 2 inches of water and place the pan on the bottom rack of the oven. Place the two foil-wrapped rib packages on an oven rack situated right above the pan filled with water and roast for 3 hours. Make sure to check on the water level every hour or so and refill as needed.

Glaze

Remove both rib packages and the water-filled roasting pan from the oven and increase the oven temperature to 450°F.

In a small mixing bowl, combine the honey with the adobo sauce until well blended. Set aside.

Carefully remove the foil and plastic wrap from the rib racks and place the racks on a baking sheet lined with foil. Making sure the bony sides of the racks are facing up, brush half of the honey glaze over them. Roast for 10 minutes.

Turn the racks over, brush with half the remaining glaze, and roast for another 5 minutes.

Brush the rest of the glaze over the rib rack and return to the oven for a final 5 minutes, or until the ribs are a dark golden brown.

Remove the ribs from the oven and allow them to rest for 10 minutes before slicing into individual ribs.

Serve

Transfer the ribs to a serving platter and serve.

ADVANCE PREPARATION The longer you marinate the ribs, the more flavorful they will be. Ideally you should marinate them for 24 hours.

You can roast the ribs a few hours before you plan to serve them and keep them wrapped in the foil until you are ready to glaze.

A pound of crab can be costly, but Castro stretches the seafood with tomatoes, onion and cilantro, then spoons it over crispy tostada shells for a refreshing appetizer that generously serves eight.

CRAB TOSTADAS

SERVES 8

- 1 pound lump crabmeat
- 1 tablespoon olive oil
- 2 tablespoons mayonnaise
- 3 tablespoons finely chopped red onion
- 1 jalapeño, stemmed and finely chopped
- 3 plum tomatoes, cored, seeded, and chopped
- ¼ cup lightly packed cilantro leaves, chopped
- 2 limes, finely grated zest and juice

Salt and black pepper

- 8 flat tostada shells, packaged (6 to 9 inches wide, round, and flat) or homemade (see Author's Note)
- 1 avocado, pitted and thinly sliced

GARNISH

Cilantro sprigs
- 2 limes, quartered

EDITOR'S WINE CHOICE

Tropical-fruited, floral Chenin Blanc: 2009 Mulderbosch

AUTHOR'S NOTE

To make tostadas, purchase 6-inch corn tortillas. Pour 2 inches of oil into a shallow pan and heat over medium-high heat. Add the tortillas, one at a time, and fry until golden brown on both sides. Place on a paper towel–lined dish and sprinkle with salt.

I often wonder if tostadas—crisp tortillas mounded with your choice of topping—were the first version of modern-day nachos. If so, these would definitely be called "supreme."

Prepare the crabmeat

Put the crabmeat in a bowl. Pick through it with your fingers to remove any cartilage.

Combine the ingredients

Add the oil, mayonnaise, onion, jalapeño, tomatoes, cilantro, and lime zest and juice to the crabmeat. Using a rubber spatula or spoon, gently fold (or toss) all ingredients until well blended. Season well with salt and pepper.

Assemble and serve

Top each tostada shell with a few slices of avocado, place a generous serving of the crabmeat mixture over it, and garnish with a sprig of cilantro. Serve each with a lime wedge.

ADVANCE PREPARATION The crabmeat mixture can be made a day in advance and refrigerated in an airtight container.

SERVING SUGGESTIONS While these tostadas make a great first course, you can also make smaller, bite-size ones to be served as hors d'oeuvres. Another more casual option is to put the crabmeat mixture in a bowl or platter and serve the tortillas alongside, allowing your guests to make their own tostadas. In this case, dice the avocado and fold it into the crabmeat mixture.

A shrimp salad like this one is appealing because it's not weighed down with mayonnaise: It's vividly flavored with lime juice and cilantro. An unexpected corn-nut topping adds crunch.

CHILLED SHRIMP & LIME SALAD

SERVES 6

- 1 pound shrimp, peeled, deveined, and butterflied (see Butterflying Shrimp)
- 1 cup cherry tomatoes, quartered
- 1 red bell pepper, thinly sliced
- ¼ red onion, thinly sliced (about ½ cup)
- 1 cup lightly packed fresh cilantro leaves, chopped, plus sprigs for garnish
- 1 jalapeño, stemmed and finely chopped
- 1 avocado, pitted and chopped
- 1 teaspoon salt, or more to taste

Black pepper
- 7 limes
- 1 tablespoon prepared horseradish
- 1 tablespoon ketchup
- 2 tablespoons olive oil

Corn nuts, for garnish

This is a wonderfully refreshing salad that walks the line between a shrimp cocktail and a ceviche. It's also incredibly forgiving—so feel free to use as much (or little) of the ingredients as you like. Tangy and fresh, it is a great start to any meal.

Blanch the shrimp

Bring a pot of salted water to a boil. Meanwhile, prepare an ice bath by filling a bowl with ice and cold water.

Add the shrimp to the boiling water and allow to cook for 1 minute. Remove the shrimp from the pot with a slotted spoon and immediately plunge into the ice bath. Allow the shrimp to cool thoroughly, then drain and place on paper towels to absorb some of the water. Transfer the shrimp to a bowl.

Prepare the vegetables

Add the tomatoes, red pepper, onion, cilantro, jalapeño, and avocado to the shrimp. Season with salt and pepper and toss lightly.

Prepare the dressing

Finely grate the zest of 3 of the limes (see Author's Note) and juice 6 limes. Combine the zest and juice in a small bowl. Mix in the horseradish, ketchup, and olive oil. Pour this dressing over the shrimp salad and toss well. Check seasoning and adjust if necessary.

AUTHOR'S NOTE

The zest of citrus fruit is the outermost layer of the fruit's skin. It adds an incredible burst of flavor and color to recipes. Use a box grater, rasp, or citrus zester to remove the skin. Make sure to remove only the colored part of the peel; the white pith is a bit bitter.

Garnish and serve

Slice the remaining lime into wedges. Transfer the salad to a serving platter and garnish with sprigs of cilantro and lime wedges. Sprinkle corn nuts over the salad for added crunch.

ADVANCE PREPARATION This salad can be prepared several hours ahead of time, which will allow the flavors to blend well. If you are preparing the salad in advance, add the salt and cilantro right before serving. Marinating the salad with the salt will toughen the shrimp and cause the vegetables to go limp. Adding the cilantro at the end will ensure that it keeps its texture and will not become too soggy.

Butterflying Shrimp

A butterflied shrimp is a shrimp that has been sliced lengthwise. In some cases, one side of the shrimp is kept attached, but other times it is sliced all the way through. For this recipe, the shrimp will be sliced in half all the way through.

Peel and devein the shrimp. Place a shrimp on your cutting board and hold your knife blade along the indentation found along the back of the shrimp (the site of the deveining). Slice the shrimp in half lengthwise using the indentation as your guide.

Preparing the shrimp in this manner before blanching will give the shrimp a nice shape after they have been cooked. It will also allow them to cook and cool quickly, thereby preventing them from becoming rubbery.

The spice level in this stew is exactly right—not too hot, not too mild—but what makes the dish so good is the deep flavor it gets from a double dose of pork: pork shoulder and fresh Mexican chorizo.

SHREDDED PORK STEW WITH CHIPOTLE TOMATO SAUCE

SERVES 6

- 1 pound pork shoulder (see Author's Note on p. 156)
- 2 bay leaves
- 3 cloves garlic, 2 crushed and 1 chopped
- 2 tablespoons olive oil
- 1 pound fresh Mexican chorizo, homemade or store-bought, casing removed
- 1 onion, sliced
- 1 teaspoon salt
- 1½ pounds (about 7) plum tomatoes, halved lengthwise, cored, and sliced
- 2 canned chipotle chiles, chopped (see Author's Note below)
- ¼ cup adobo sauce from canned chipotles
- ½ teaspoon dried oregano
- 2 sprigs fresh thyme, leaves removed from stem
- 2 sprigs fresh marjoram, leaves removed from stem

GARNISH
- 6 sprigs cilantro
Tortilla chips
Mexican *crema,* homemade or store-bought

AUTHOR'S NOTE

Chipotles are smoked jalapeños and have the heat of a jalapeño, but you can remove the seeds found in the chile if you want to reduce the heat.

This is an incredibly satisfying stew that gets better as it ages, so think about making extra to keep as leftovers. The smoky chipotles add a depth of flavor along with a spicy heat. To tame the heat, you can reduce the number of chipotles or serve the stew with Mexican crema.

Prepare the meat

Put the pork in a saucepan and fill with enough water to cover the meat by 1 inch. Add the bay leaves and crushed garlic. Bring to a boil and skim off the grayish foam that rises to the top during the first few minutes. Decrease the heat to a simmer and cook for 45 minutes, partially covered, or until the pork is tender.

Allow the pork to cool in the stock, then drain, reserving 1 cup of the stock. Shred the pork by pulling apart the fibers with your fingers. Set aside.

Prepare the chorizo

Heat 1 tablespoon of the olive oil in a saucepan over medium heat. Add the chorizo to the pan and cook, breaking it apart as you stir, until it achieves a golden brown color and begins to render its fat. (Don't worry if some of the chorizo sticks to the bottom of the pan.) Using a slotted spoon, remove the chorizo from the pan and set it aside.

continued on p. 156

EDITOR'S WINE CHOICE

**Rich, berry-scented Syrah:
2007 R Wines Strong Arms Shiraz**

AUTHOR'S NOTE

You need a fatty cut of meat for this recipe, so if you cannot find shoulder, the only other cut to use is pork butt. A lean cut will result in tough and dry pork. You can easily substitute beef flank steak for the pork. The beef only needs to be simmered for 30 minutes, but cooks the same as the pork after that.

Brown the main ingredients

Add the remaining 1 tablespoon olive oil to the unwashed pan and set it over medium heat. Add the onion and remaining chopped garlic and sauté until the onion begins to get limp and translucent, 3 minutes. Add the shredded pork, season with the salt, and continue sautéing for 3 more minutes. Deglaze the pan by pouring in a couple of tablespoons of the reserved pork stock and scraping the bottom of the pan with a heatproof silicone spatula.

Finish the stew

Add the chorizo, tomatoes, chipotles, adobo from canned chipotles, oregano, thyme leaves, and marjoram leaves to the pan. Stir well and simmer for 5 minutes. Pour in the remaining reserved pork stock and continue simmering, uncovered, for 25 minutes.

Garnish and serve

Pour the finished stew into a large shallow bowl and garnish with sprigs of cilantro. Serve with tortilla chips and Mexican *crema*.

ADVANCE PREPARATION This dish improves with age as its flavors really blend. You can make this recipe up to 1 day in advance.

While working on her next book, about Latin grilling, Castro created these mini chorizo burgers—a sweet-spicy answer to the sloppy joe, topped with guava ketchup and fried potato sticks.

CHORIZO SLIDERS

MAKES 12 SLIDERS

- ½ small onion, coarsely chopped
- 1 garlic clove
- 1 tablespoon hot paprika
- 1 tablespoon smoked sweet paprika
- 1 teaspoon ground cumin
- ½ cup ketchup
- 2½ tablespoons Worcestershire sauce
- 2½ teaspoons kosher salt
- ¾ pound ground beef chuck
- ¼ pound ground pork
- Vegetable oil, for frying
- 1 baking potato (about 10 ounces)—peeled, coarsely grated and patted dry
- ¼ cup guava or apricot jelly
- 12 small potato rolls, split

EDITOR'S WINE CHOICE

Spicy, blackberry-flavored Zinfandel: 2007 Ravenswood Sonoma County Old Vine

1. Make the patties: In the bowl of a food processor, combine the onion, garlic, hot paprika, smoked sweet paprika and cumin with ¼ cup of the ketchup, 2 tablespoons of the Worcestershire sauce and the salt; puree until smooth. Scrape the puree into a large bowl. Add the meats and mix until evenly combined. Form the meat into twelve ½-inch-thick patties and transfer to a plate. Cover and refrigerate for 1 hour.

2. Meanwhile, in a large saucepan, heat 1 inch of oil until it registers 350°F on a deep-fry thermometer. In small batches, sprinkle the potato into the hot oil and fry, stirring occasionally, until golden, about 1 minute. Using a slotted spoon, transfer the potato sticks to a paper towel–lined plate to drain. Season with salt.

3. In a small bowl, stir the guava jelly with the remaining ¼ cup of ketchup and ½ tablespoon of Worcestershire sauce.

4. Heat a grill pan. Grill the chorizo patties over moderately high heat until slightly pink in the centers, about 3 minutes per side. Spread the guava ketchup on both sides of the buns. Mound half of the potato sticks on the bottom buns and top with the chorizo patties. Mound the remaining potato sticks on the patties, close the sliders and serve.

NOTE These sliders are not hard to make, but to simplify them even more, substitute store-bought potato sticks for homemade.

MAKE AHEAD The sliders can be prepared through Step 1 and refrigerated overnight.

LOURDES CASTRO ONLINE
lourdes-castro.com
f Lourdes Castro
t @LourdesCastro

CARAMELIZED ONIONS WITH
IDIAZÁBAL CHEESE, P. 160

PINTXOS

Gerald Hirigoyen with Lisa Weiss

Chef Gerald Hirigoyen brought Basque tapas, or *pintxos* (PEEN-chos), to his acclaimed San Francisco restaurants; now, he brings the one- or two-bite dishes to the pages of a book. Hirigoyen's take on Basque cooking—a beguiling combination of seafood from the Bay of Biscay and earthy ingredients like chorizo and potatoes—is meant to evoke the experience of *ir de tapeo* (going from one tapas bar to the next). He recommends making a meal of little dishes, perhaps preparing chicken with Basque "ketchup" (made with peppers and vinegar), clam chowder and caramelized onions with smoked Idiazábal cheese. Add serrano ham and piquillo peppers from the market, and "before you know it," Hirigoyen writes, "you will have a party."

Published by Ten Speed Press, $24.95

These fast, easy hors d'oeuvres are particularly fun to eat. If you can't find Idiazábal, opt for Manchego or a firm pecorino. To serve, look for pretty skewers to hold the crisp onions and creamy cheese.

CARAMELIZED ONIONS WITH IDIAZÁBAL CHEESE

MAKES 8 SKEWERS

- 16 red pearl onions
- ¼ cup dry sherry
- 1 tablespoon plus 1 teaspoon sugar
- 8 squares Idiazábal cheese, 1 inch square and ⅓ inch thick

Piment d'Espelette for finishing

EDITOR'S WINE CHOICE

Fruity, lively sparkling rosé:
2006 Llopart Rosé Brut Cava

Idiazábal, a smoked Basque sheep's milk cheese with a tangy, somewhat sweet flavor, has become quite popular in cheese markets. It marries particularly well with the caramelized onions in this recipe.

Have ready a small bowl of ice water. Bring a small saucepan filled with water to a boil over high heat, add the onions, and boil for 1 minute. Drain and plunge into the ice water until cool. Cut off the root ends and slip off the skins.

Return the onions to the saucepan and add the sherry, sugar, and water just to cover. Bring to a boil over high heat, decrease the heat to medium, and cook, swirling the pan occasionally, for about 10 minutes, or until the onions are tender when pierced with a small knife and the liquid is syrupy and reduced to 2 to 3 tablespoons. Watch carefully, lowering the heat and adding a little water if necessary to prevent scorching. Using a slotted spoon, transfer the onions to a plate. Reserve the syrup in the pan.

To serve, have ready 8 small bamboo skewers. Thread 1 onion, 1 cheese square, and a second onion onto each skewer, and arrange the skewers on a small platter. Drizzle with the reserved syrup, and sprinkle with a little Piment d'Espelette.

This chowder full of clams, potatoes and peppers can be served in small portions as part of a tapas spread, but it's also hearty enough to serve as a light main course with grilled bread and a salad.

BASQUE CLAM CHOWDER

MAKES ABOUT EIGHT 1-CUP SERVINGS

CLAMS
- ¼ cup extra-virgin olive oil
- 3 garlic cloves, lightly smashed
- ¼ cup finely diced onion
- 1 cup dry vermouth or white wine
- 4 pounds Manila clams, scrubbed

- 2 tablespoons olive oil
- ¼ pound salt pork, cut into strips 1 inch long by ¼ inch thick and wide
- ¾ cup ½-inch-dice onion
- 6 garlic cloves, lightly smashed
- 1 red bell pepper, cored, seeded, and cut into ¼-inch dice
- 1 yellow bell pepper, cored, seeded, and cut into ¼-inch dice
- 4 cups Chicken Stock (recipe follows) or good-quality commercial chicken stock
- Bouquet garni of 5 or 6 sprigs thyme, 1 bay leaf, and 6 to 8 sprigs flat-leaf parsley wrapped in a cheesecloth sachet or tied with kitchen twine
- 2½ cups ½-inch-dice peeled russet potatoes
- Kosher salt and freshly ground black pepper

The Basque Country shares the beautiful, rugged Spanish coastline of the Bay of Biscay with the regions of Cantabria, Asturias, and Galicia to the west. Some of the finest seafood in the world is fished here, and I created this clam-rich recipe to echo the kind of sopa *you might find on a menu in San Sebastián: simple, hearty, and tasting of the essence of the sea and of earthy Basque peppers and potatoes. It is easy to prepare, appreciated by everyone who likes a good chowder, and perfect in tapas-size portions for entertaining or larger portions for a weeknight supper main course.*

To cook the clams, heat a large casserole or Dutch oven over high heat until hot. Add the extra-virgin olive oil and warm it until it ripples. Add the garlic and onion and cook, stirring occasionally, for about 3 minutes, or until lightly colored. Add the vermouth and the clams and cook, uncovered, for 3 to 5 minutes, or until the clams have opened. Remove from the heat. Using a slotted spoon, transfer the clams to a bowl, discarding any that failed to open. Pour the cooking liquid through a fine-mesh sieve lined with cheesecloth into a glass measuring cup. You should have 1 to 1¼ cups. Set the casserole aside. When the clams are cool enough to handle, remove them from their shells and coarsely chop the meats. Set the chopped clams and cooking liquid aside separately.

continued on p. 162

PINTXOS
Gerald Hirigoyen with Lisa Weiss

To make the soup base, return the same casserole to medium-high heat and heat until hot. Add the olive oil and warm it until it ripples. Add the salt pork, onion, and garlic and cook, stirring occasionally, for 3 to 4 minutes, or until the fat has rendered from the salt pork and the onion has begun to color. Add the bell peppers, decrease the heat to medium, and continue to cook, stirring occasionally, for 8 minutes more. Add the reserved clam cooking liquid, stock, and bouquet garni, increase the heat to high, and bring to a boil. Add the potatoes, decrease the heat to maintain a simmer, and cook for about 10 minutes, or until the potatoes are tender. Season to taste with salt and pepper. (At this point, the soup base can be covered and set aside at room temperature for up to 4 hours or refrigerated for up to 2 days.)

To serve, reheat the soup base to a simmer if necessary. Add the reserved clams and remove from the heat. Ladle into warmed soup bowls.

CHICKEN STOCK

MAKES ABOUT 3 QUARTS

- 4 pounds chicken wings, legs, backs, or carcasses
- 1 large carrot, cut into 1-inch pieces
- 2 celery stalks, cut into 1-inch pieces
- 1 large onion, cut into quarters
- Bouquet garni of 2 to 4 sprigs thyme, 1 bay leaf, and 12 sprigs flat-leaf parsley wrapped in cheesecloth or tied with kitchen twine
- 1 teaspoon black peppercorns

Commercial broth, the kind on grocery-store shelves, is great to have on hand to use in a pinch, but if you want a dish to sing, nothing beats using homemade stock. I buy chicken pieces, particularly wings, when they are on sale at the market, and I also try to accumulate carcasses in the freezer. Sometimes I add a few chicken feet or even a halved calf's foot to the pot to give the finished stock more viscosity.

In a stockpot, combine the chicken pieces with water to cover by 3 inches. Bring to a boil over high heat, immediately decrease the heat to maintain a low simmer, and skim off and discard any foam or other impurities that form on the surface. Maintaining a low simmer, add the carrot, celery, onion, bouquet garni, and peppercorns. Cook uncovered, skimming as needed, for 3 to 4 hours, or until well flavored.

Strain the stock through a fine-mesh sieve into a clean container, let cool completely, and refrigerate until the fat has solidified on the surface (after several hours), at which time the fat will be easier to remove and discard. The stock can be covered and refrigerated for up to 4 days or frozen for up to 2 months. If the stock has been refrigerated, it can then be brought back to a boil, cooled, covered, and refrigerated for 2 days longer.

PINTXOS
Gerald Hirigoyen with Lisa Weiss

After cooking chicken in a delightful sweet-sour sauce, Hirigoyen takes the extra step of crisping the skin under the broiler.

CHICKEN THIGHS WITH SPICY BASQUE "KETCHUP"

SERVES 4

- 4 skin-on chicken thighs
- Kosher salt and freshly ground black pepper
- 2 tablespoons olive oil
- 2 tablespoons dark brown sugar
- ¼ cup sherry vinegar
- 1 heaping cup Pipérade (recipe follows), pureed
- 2 teaspoons Piment d'Espelette
- Chopped fresh flat-leaf parsley for garnish

It is the addictive sauce that makes this dish special. Sweet from the peppers and brown sugar, spicy from the Piment d'Espelette, and tangy from the vinegar, the sauce is easy to put together, can be made in quantity (this recipe makes three-quarter cup but can be increased easily three or four times), and is good with everything from these chicken thighs to eggs and fried potatoes.

Preheat the broiler.

Sprinkle the chicken on all sides with salt and pepper. Heat a sauté pan over high heat until hot. Add the olive oil and warm it until it ripples. Add the chicken, skin side down, and cook for 3 to 4 minutes, or until the skin is golden brown. Using tongs, turn and cook on the second side for 3 minutes, or until lightly browned. Transfer the chicken to a plate and discard the oil.

Return the pan to high heat and add the brown sugar, whisking until it melts. Remove from the heat and whisk in the sherry vinegar. Return the pan to medium heat and whisk the mixture for about 1 minute, or until it has thickened and reduced. Stir in the *pipérade* and the Piment d'Espelette. Return the chicken to the pan, cover, decrease the heat to low, and cook for 10 minutes, or until the thighs are cooked through.

Transfer the chicken, skin side up, to a broiler pan and broil for about 2 minutes, or until the skin is crisp.

To serve, spoon a pool of the sauce on each warmed plate and top with a chicken thigh. Sprinkle with the parsley.

PIPÉRADE

MAKES 3 CUPS

⅓ cup olive oil

1 small onion, thinly sliced lengthwise

1 red bell pepper, cored, seeded, and cut lengthwise into ¼-inch-wide strips

1 yellow bell pepper, cored, seeded, and cut lengthwise into ¼-inch-wide strips

6 garlic cloves, crushed or thinly sliced

4 ripe tomatoes, cored and cut into rough ¾-inch cubes

Kosher salt

Piment d'Espelette

AUTHOR'S WINE CHOICE

The Navarre region is in north-central Spain, and its food is strongly influenced by the Basque Country, which borders it. Most of the grapes grown there are Garnacha, and though it was long thought of as the region of *rosadas,* or rosés, its reds are gaining in popularity. A spry, light, fruity Navarre red, served slightly chilled, is ideal here.

Pipérade *is basically a stew of sweet peppers and onions and is the quintessential dish of the Basque country.*

Heat a large sauté pan over medium-high heat until hot. Add the olive oil and warm it until it ripples. Add the onion, bell peppers, garlic, and tomatoes and cook, stirring occasionally, for about 10 minutes, or until the vegetables have softened and have begun to color. Remove from the heat and let cool.

Season to taste with salt and Piment d'Espelette before using, and then use immediately, or store in a tightly covered container in the refrigerator for up to 5 days.

PINTXOS
Gerald Hirigoyen with Lisa Weiss

These elegant quail are perfect for a dinner party. They marinate in a fantastic mix of spices, brown sugar, orange zest, garlic and shallot, then cook on the stove in less than 10 minutes.

SPICED BUTTERFLIED QUAIL ELCANO

SERVES 4

- 1 teaspoon coriander seeds
- 3 cardamom pods
- 1 teaspoon black peppercorns
- 2 garlic cloves, thinly sliced
- 1 large shallot, thinly sliced
- Grated zest of 1 small orange
- ¼ teaspoon ground cinnamon
- Pinch of ground mace
- Pinch of ground cloves
- 1 tablespoon dark brown sugar
- ¼ cup extra-virgin olive oil
- 4 boneless quail
- Fleur de sel or other coarse salt

AUTHOR'S WINE CHOICE

You need a full, fruity red here to stand up to the sweet spices, such as a Pinot Noir from Monterey, California's Miura Vineyards. It has lots of cherry, berry, and plum flavors and a bit of spice to match the marinade seasoning.

AUTHOR'S NOTE

This recipe calls for boneless quail that have had their backbones and rib cages removed. You may need to special order them fresh or frozen (which does not affect quality). If you are unsure about cooking them, just remember to do it quickly. Quail are best eaten when their juices run a little pink.

Although not as famous as his Portuguese commander, Ferdinand Magellan, navigator Juan Sebastián Elcano was one of many Basque sailors who joined Magellan on his voyage in search of spices in the Moluccas. He became captain of the expedition after Magellan was killed in the Philippines, guiding the diminished expedition back to Spain and completing the first circumnavigation of the globe. The use of the spices in this recipe—cinnamon, cloves, coriander, and cardamom—are my tribute to Elcano.

Using a mortar and pestle or the bottom edge of a heavy pan, crush the coriander, cardamom seeds (removed from their pods), and peppercorns to a coarse powder. Pour into a small bowl and add the garlic, shallot, orange zest, cinnamon, mace, cloves, brown sugar, and olive oil. Mix well.

If using boneless quail, cut each quail down its back and spread it out so it lies flat. If using bone-in quail, split them along the backbone and press flat. Rub the spice mixture over the entire surface of each quail. Then cover and marinate in the refrigerator for at least 4 hours or up to overnight.

To cook the quail, heat a griddle, cast-iron skillet, or sauté pan over high heat until very hot. Decrease the heat to medium-high, add the quail, skin side down, and cook for about 4 minutes, or until browned. Using tongs, turn and cook on the second side for about 4 minutes, or until browned.

To serve, transfer the birds to a warmed serving platter and sprinkle with the fleur de sel.

A clafoutis is a French dessert made by pouring sweet batter over fresh fruit, then baking it. The pineapple here—broiled until it's wonderfully caramelized—is a fun alternative to the usual cherries.

PINEAPPLE CLAFOUTIS

SERVES 8

- ½ medium pineapple—peeled, quartered, cored and sliced crosswise ¼ inch thick
- 2 tablespoons unsalted butter, cut into 8 pieces
- 2 tablespoons packed dark brown sugar
- 4 large eggs, at room temperature
- ⅓ cup granulated sugar
- ½ vanilla bean, split, seeds scraped
- 2 tablespoons all-purpose flour
- ¾ cup heavy cream
- 1 teaspoon finely grated orange zest
- 1 teaspoon finely grated lemon zest

Confectioners' sugar, for dusting

1. Preheat the broiler. In a 9½-inch round ceramic or glass baking dish, arrange the pineapple in concentric circles. Dot the pineapple with the butter and sprinkle with the brown sugar. Broil the pineapple 3 inches from the heat, rotating the dish if necessary, until the pineapple is lightly browned all over, about 8 minutes.

2. Preheat the oven to 425°F. In a large bowl, using a handheld mixer, beat the eggs with the granulated sugar and vanilla seeds at medium-high speed until airy and slightly thickened, about 2 minutes. Add the flour and beat until just incorporated. Add the cream, orange zest and lemon zest and beat at medium speed until thickened and frothy, about 1 minute. Pour the batter over the pineapple.

3. Bake the clafoutis for about 20 minutes, until the top is golden and the custard is set. Let cool for 15 minutes. Dust with confectioners' sugar and serve warm or at room temperature.

GERALD HIRIGOYEN ONLINE

bocasf.com

f Gerald Hirigoyen

t @gizon

MAUI-STYLE SNAPPER, P. 170

TACOS

Mark Miller with Benjamin Hargett & Jane Horn

Heading to a taco truck is one way (admittedly, a fantastic and increasingly popular way) to get a Mexican street-food fix. Cooking with this new paperback from Mark Miller, founder of Santa Fe's Coyote Café, is another. A pioneer of modern Southwestern cuisine, Miller shares both taco-stand classics like shredded pork tacos and more creative ideas like a luxe lobster-and-avocado version—all perfect party food. To create a salsa bar for entertaining, Miller outlines his "basic seven": One raw salsa, one cooked, pickled vegetables, *crema* (Mexican crème fraîche), cilantro, white onion and limes. Have all the elements ready in advance, he says, and you're thinking like the best *taqueros* (taco masters), who can put together a spectacular taco in seconds.

Published by Ten Speed Press, $21.95

TACOS
Mark Miller with Benjamin Hargett
& Jane Horn

What makes this simple grilled-fish taco stand out is the
sweet and spicy habanero-glazed pineapple that gets piled
onto the tortilla with the meaty strips of lime-marinated fish.

MAUI-STYLE SNAPPER

MAKES 8 TACOS
HEAT LEVEL 3 OUT OF 10
PREP TIME 30 MINUTES

1   small pineapple, peeled,
    cored, and sliced into rings
¼   cup habanero hot sauce or
    Tabasco sauce
½   cup vegetable oil
2   tablespoons fresh lime juice
1   tablespoon fine sea salt
1½ pounds boneless, skinless red
    snapper or mahi mahi fillets,
    cut into 2½-by-½-inch strips
Eight 5½-inch soft white or yellow
    corn tortillas, for serving

GARNISH
Iceberg Lettuce Garnish
    (recipe follows) and
    avocado wedges

AUTHOR'S DRINK CHOICE

Margaritas, coco locos

*Unlike Baja fish tacos, which are deep-fried in batter, those
made Maui-style are grilled. One of my funniest fish taco
experiences occurred in a small town in Alaska where we had
stopped for supplies during a sailing trip through Prince
William Sound. There in front of us was an old school bus
painted in bright, tropical colors now converted to a walk-up
kitchen selling, of all things—Maui tacos! We were a long
way from Hawaii, but the methods were the same—the local
catch (salmon and crab, in this case), simply grilled and
served with salsa on fresh tortillas.*

Prepare a charcoal or gas grill. In a large bowl, toss the
pineapple with the hot sauce. Grill the fruit slices over very low
heat until browned and caramelized, 10 minutes per side
(don't let the slices blacken or burn). Cut the pineapple rings
into small wedges and set aside.

Meanwhile, in a large bowl, combine the oil, lime juice, and salt
and marinate the snapper strips in the mixture for 5 minutes
(the oil will help prevent the fish from sticking to the grill). Once
the pineapple is done, grill the fish over medium-high heat until
cooked through, turning once, about 6 minutes total. Remove
from the grill and serve immediately.

To serve, lay the tortillas side by side, open face and overlapping
on a platter. Divide the lettuce, fish, pineapple, and avocado
equally between the tortillas and top with salsa. Grab, fold, and
eat right away. Or build your own taco: lay a tortilla, open face,
in one hand. Spoon on lettuce, filling, avocado, and salsa, and eat.

ICEBERG LETTUCE GARNISH

MAKES 3 CUPS, ENOUGH FOR 12 TACOS
HEAT LEVEL 4 OUT OF 10
PREP TIME 15 MINUTES

½   head medium (6-inch diameter)
     iceberg lettuce
½   cup Salsa Fresca (recipe follows)

Line a bowl with paper towels and have ready. Remove the outer leaves of the lettuce. Cut a V-shaped wedge around the inner core and remove the core and discard. Halve the lettuce to make 2 quarter sections. With a large, sharp knife, slice each section crosswise into a very, very thin julienne or julienne with a hand-held Japanese mandoline. Transfer the julienned lettuce to the paper towel–lined bowl to absorb any excess water exuded by the lettuce when sliced. Discard the paper towels, and in the same bowl, toss the lettuce with salsa and use immediately, or the lettuce will wilt.

SALSA FRESCA

MAKES 4 CUPS
HEAT LEVEL 5 OUT OF 10
PREP TIME 30 MINUTES

12   small, ripe Roma tomatoes
     (about 1½ pounds), cut into
     ¼-inch dice
2   serrano chiles, seeded and minced
½   small red onion, cut into
     ⅛-inch dice
     Leaves from 1 bunch cilantro, finely
     chopped
1   tablespoon fresh lime juice
¾   teaspoon kosher salt
¼   teaspoon sugar

Here is the recipe used at the Coyote Café. Along with chopped onions, fresh cilantro, salsa tomatillo, and red chile sauce, it's always offered as a basic condiment with tacos, regardless of whatever special salsa is paired with a particular taco filling. Salsa fresca is used in Mexico like we use ketchup—to wake up plain foods. But salsa fresca is better than ketchup because it is made fresh—ripe tomatoes, a bit of onion for crunch, the heat of green chile, the tang of fresh lime juice, and the refreshing lift of aromatic cilantro.

In a large bowl, mix all ingredients together and serve. This salsa is best used the day it's made or the tomatoes become watery.

TACOS
*Mark Miller with Benjamin Hargett
& Jane Horn*

The filling for these tacos is a spicy and fresh-tasting pork stew made with pork shoulder, chiles, onion, garlic and cilantro. A squirt of fresh lime juice would punch up the flavor.

GREEN CHILE PORK MONDONGO

MAKES 8 TACOS
HEAT LEVEL 7 OUT OF 10
PREP TIME 1 HOUR 20 MINUTES

1 poblano chile, oil-roasted, peeled, cored, and seeded (see To Oil-Roast Fresh Chiles)
3 tablespoons vegetable oil, plus more for refrying
½ white onion, cut into ¼-inch dice
1¼ pounds pork shoulder, cut into 1-inch cubes
4 cups water
2 serrano chiles, dry-roasted, stemmed, and seeded (see To Dry-Roast Fresh Chiles)
1 garlic clove, dry-roasted (see To Dry-Roast Garlic)
Leaves from 1 bunch cilantro
Kosher salt and freshly ground black pepper
Eight 5½-inch soft white corn tortillas, for serving

GARNISH
Avocado cubes or strips of roasted poblano or jalapeño chiles

AUTHOR'S DRINK CHOICE

Mexican beer (such as Pacifico)

Mondongo is usually a thick, spicy stew made with beef tripe and lots of locally grown vegetables, probably Spanish in origin. You can find many versions of it throughout Latin America and the Caribbean. The one I am most familiar with was prepared by our wonderful Mexican chef Daniel Alvarez, who cooked at the Coyote Cantina for over twenty years. His version used pork butt instead of tripe, lots of green chiles, sometimes posole or corn, and other green vegetables. He made this dish often for the staff meal and sometimes as a special at the Cantina. It always sold out quickly.

Cut the prepared poblano chiles into ¼-inch-thick strips (rajas); set aside.

In a skillet, heat 1 tablespoon of the oil over medium-high heat and sauté the onion until it begins to caramelize, about 5 minutes; set aside.

In a large, heavy nonstick skillet, heat the remaining 2 tablespoons of oil over high heat and sauté the pork cubes until browned, about 15 minutes. Decrease heat to medium-low, add 1 cup of the water, and simmer until tender, about 1 hour, adding 1 cup of the water every 15 minutes after the last cup of water has cooked off so the pan doesn't dry out.

Meanwhile, in the jar of a blender, add the reserved chile strips, sautéed onion, garlic, and cilantro and puree until smooth. Season with salt and pepper.

When the pork is tender and all the water in the skillet has dried up, add enough oil to fill the pan bottom about ⅛ inch and heat over high heat until almost smoking. Add the chile puree sauce to the pan with the pork, remove from the heat, and stir to blend. Serve immediately or remove from the heat, cover, and keep warm at room temperature up to 3 to 4 hours. Reheat gently when ready to serve.

To serve, lay the tortillas side by side, open face and overlapping on a platter. Divide the filling equally between the tortillas and top with salsa. Grab, fold, and eat right away. Or build your own taco: lay a tortilla, open face, in one hand. Spoon on some filling, top with salsa, and eat right away.

To Oil-Roast Fresh Chiles

In a heavy-bottomed pan, heat 2 inches of canola oil to 375°F. Carefully add 1 or 2 whole chiles to the hot oil (roast just a few at a time so they don't crowd each other and lower the temperature of the oil). Turn them as the submerged part of the chiles begins to blister, 1½ minutes per side. Turn the chiles as necessary until all sides are blistered, but not burned. **Do not wash the chiles after roasting or you'll lose flavor.**

To Dry-Roast Fresh Chiles

Heat a dry cast-iron or heavy-bottomed skillet or flat griddle over medium heat. Place the chiles in the hot pan and cook, turning every 5 minutes, until all sides are evenly blistered. The skin can char a bit, but the goal is to loosen the skin, but keep it intact, and cook the flesh partially without it breaking down and becoming too soft.

To Dry-Roast Garlic

In a dry cast-iron or heavy-bottomed skillet, place unpeeled garlic cloves and dry-roast over low heat until the garlic softens, 30 to 40 minutes. Shake the pan occasionally. Or, roast garlic cloves in a preheated 350°F oven until soft, 20 to 30 minutes. When done, the garlic should be creamy and sweet, and soft enough to slip out of the skin when you squeeze the clove.

Here's a great vegetarian taco, with portobello mushrooms in place of meat. Two ingredients add a nice smokiness: chipotle puree stirred into the mushrooms, and smoked mozzarella sprinkled on top.

PORTOBELLO MUSHROOMS WITH CHIPOTLE

MAKES 8 TACOS
HEAT LEVEL 3 OUT OF 10
PREP TIME 25 MINUTES

- 1 pound portobello mushrooms (preferably small, with fresh, closed gills)
- 3 tablespooons (or more) unsalted butter
- 3 cloves garlic, minced
- ½ teaspoon kosher salt
- Pinch of freshly ground black pepper
- 2 teaspoons chipotle puree (See To Make Chipotle Puree)
- 1 tablespoon finely chopped fresh cilantro leaves
- 1 cup finely grated smoked mozzarella or smoked gouda cheese (about 4 ounces)
- Eight 5½-inch soft yellow corn tortillas, for serving

GARNISH
Lightly toasted pine nuts
   or pumpkin seeds

AUTHOR'S DRINK CHOICE

Dark beer, Tempranillo

Remove the mushroom stems, chop them, and reserve. If any of the mushrooms are large, scrape off the gills with a spoon and reserve. Cut the caps into ¼-inch-thick slices and reserve.

Preheat a heavy skillet large enough to hold the mushrooms in a single layer for about 2 minutes over medium-high heat. Melt the butter in the pan, then add the sliced mushroom caps, chopped stems, any reserved gills, minced garlic, salt, and pepper, and sauté until golden brown and caramelized, 8 to 10 minutes. You may need to cook the mushrooms in batches to be sure they brown and not steam from overcrowding. Add more butter as the mushrooms cook, if necessary, as they have a tendency to absorb all the butter from the pan.

Remove from the heat and mix in the chipotle puree and cilantro. Sprinkle on the cheese just to melt and serve immediately or keep warm until ready to serve.

To serve, lay the tortillas side by side, open face and overlapping on a platter. Divide the filling equally between the tortillas and top with salsa and pumpkin seeds. Grab, fold, and eat right away. Or build your own taco: lay a tortilla, open face, in one hand. Spoon on some filling, top with salsa and pine nuts, and eat right away.

To Make Chipotle Puree

Make this yourself to give a flavor boost to a variety of recipes: Puree a can of chipotles in adobo sauce in a blender and store airtight in the refrigerator for up to 1 month.

Adding figs to thick, luscious mole—made with plenty of spicy chiles—gives the sauce a good, fruity flavor. This version is super on grilled pork, but it's also great on chicken or beef.

PORK TENDERLOIN WITH FIG MOLE

8 SERVINGS

- 12 dried Mission figs (4 ounces), stems removed
- ¾ cup tawny port
- ¼ cup vegetable oil
- 1 slice of white sandwich bread
- 1 small onion, finely chopped
- 2 garlic cloves, minced
- 3 pasilla chiles, stemmed and seeded
- 2 ancho chiles, stemmed and seeded
- ¼ cup raisins
- 2 cups chicken stock or low-sodium broth
- 1½ tablespoons sherry vinegar
- 1½ tablespoons dark brown sugar
- ¼ teaspoon cinnamon
- Pinch of ground allspice
- 1 ounce bittersweet chocolate, chopped
- ⅓ cup warm water
- Kosher salt
- 4 pork tenderloins (14 ounces each)
- Freshly ground pepper

EDITOR'S WINE CHOICE

Black cherry–scented, rich Syrah: 2008 Melville Estate–Verna's

EDITOR'S NOTE

The mole can be refrigerated for up to 1 week. Reheat gently before serving, adding water to thin out the sauce if necessary.

1. In a small saucepan, combine the figs with the port. Bring to a simmer and cook over moderate heat until the port has reduced by half, about 15 minutes.

2. In a small skillet, heat 2 tablespoons of the oil. Add the bread and fry over moderately high heat until golden on both sides, about 3 minutes. Transfer to paper towels to drain.

3. In a large saucepan, heat 1 tablespoon of the oil. Add the onion and garlic and cook over moderately high heat until golden, about 8 minutes. Add the pasilla and ancho chiles, raisins, stock, vinegar, brown sugar, cinnamon, allspice, fried bread and the figs in port. Bring to a simmer and cook over low heat until the chiles are softened, about 20 minutes. Scrape the mixture into a blender and puree until smooth. Strain the mole into a medium bowl, pressing with the back of a spoon to extract as much mole as possible. Discard the solids.

4. In a large skillet, heat the remaining 1 tablespoon of oil until shimmering. Add the mole and cook over moderately high heat until the mixture darkens slightly, about 3 minutes. Remove from the heat and stir in the chocolate until melted. Add the water and season the mole with salt; keep warm.

5. Light a grill or preheat a grill pan. Season the pork with salt and pepper and grill over moderately high heat, turning once, until browned and just slightly rosy in the center, about 12 minutes total. Transfer the tenderloins to a work surface and let rest for 5 minutes. Spoon some of the mole onto plates. Thinly slice the tenderloins, arrange on the mole and serve.

WORLD FOOD

PORK CHOPS
WITH PLUMS AND
CHINESE SPICES,
P. 180

PURE SIMPLE COOKING

Diana Henry

When Diana Henry had a baby, she gained new respect for quick recipes. As a TV host and food columnist for Britain's *Sunday Telegraph,* she was better equipped than many to make speedy food interesting. The first thing she did was focus on recipes that cook in the oven—an efficient method for the multitasking cook. Then she plundered the cuisines of every country she could think of for ways to make simple recipes more exciting. The result: especially easy, globally accented dishes, such as Pork Chops with Plums and Chinese Spices. She emphasizes vegetables, seasonality and convenience with recipes like Turkish Baked Eggplant with Chile, Feta and Mint. Any busy person (new parent or not) will find much to appreciate here.

Published by Ten Speed Press, $21.95

This sweet-spicy recipe is a great one-pan dish. The chops bake in the oven with plums, honey, ginger and other Asian flavorings, which slowly glaze the meat in a sticky sauce.

PORK CHOPS WITH PLUMS & CHINESE SPICES

SERVES 4

- 1 pound plums, preferably crimson-fleshed ones
- Four 8-ounce pork chops, bone in and partly trimmed of fat
- 5 tablespoons honey
- 1 teaspoon Chinese five-spice powder
- 1 teaspoon ground ginger
- 1 medium fresh red chile, seeded and finely chopped
- 4 cloves garlic, crushed
- Juice of ½ orange
- 1 teaspoon white wine vinegar
- Salt and pepper

EDITOR'S WINE CHOICE

Spicy, cherry-rich Côtes du Rhône: 2007 M. Chapoutier Belleruche

Despite its simplicity, this dish looks so lovely—glossy with honey, crimson juices running out of the plums—that it's special enough to serve to friends. So much better than "dinner-party" food. Serve with rice and stir-fried greens or a watercress or spinach salad.

1. Preheat the oven to 375°F. Halve and pit the plums. If they are quite large, cut them into quarters or sixths; small ones need only be halved. Lay the chops in a shallow ovenproof dish and tuck the plums in around them where they can lie in a single layer without overlapping.

2. Mix together the honey, five-spice powder, ginger, chile, garlic, orange juice, vinegar, and salt and pepper. Pour over the chops and plums, turning everything to make sure all are well coated. Bake for 45 minutes, until cooked through. Serve hot.

NOTE Go to a good butcher and buy thickly cut chops that are organic, or at least from pasture-raised pigs. If the butcher sells pork from heritage breeds, even better.

Canned beans are a terrific shortcut for hearty purees like the one served with this cod. To add even more flavor to the mild fish, Henry also serves it with a tasty dressing of anchovies and parsley.

ROAST COD WITH ANCHOVIES & BEAN PUREE

SERVES 4

BEANS

- 2 tablespoons olive oil
- ½ onion, coarsely chopped
- 1 clove garlic, crushed
- Two 14-ounce cans cannellini beans, drained
- ⅔ cup chicken stock or water
- Salt and pepper
- ¼ cup extra-virgin olive oil
- A good squeeze of lemon

- One 2-ounce can anchovies, drained
- 1 tablespoon chopped fresh flat-leaf parsley
- 6 tablespoons extra-virgin olive oil
- A good squeeze of lemon
- 2 tablespoons olive oil
- Four 6-ounce cod fillets
- Salt and pepper

EDITOR'S WINE CHOICE

Fragrant, zippy Pinot Gris: 2009 Sineann

A classy dish, which succeeds because of the interplay of flavors—the sweetness of cod, the saltiness of anchovies, and the earthiness of beans. Chopped black olives can be added to the anchovy dressing (in which case add more lemon and olive oil) or replace the anchovies altogether.

1. For the beans, heat the olive oil in a saucepan and gently cook the onion until it is soft but not colored. Add the garlic, beans, stock, and salt and pepper. Cook over medium heat for about 4 minutes.

2. Process the beans and the liquid in a blender or food processor with the extra-virgin olive oil and the lemon juice. Taste and adjust the seasoning. You can set the puree aside to heat up later, or serve it at room temperature.

3. Chop the anchovies and parsley together and stir in the extra-virgin olive oil. Add a squeeze of lemon as well. Set aside.

4. Preheat the oven to 400°F. Heat the 2 tablespoons olive oil in a nonstick frying pan over medium-high heat. Lightly season the cod with salt and pepper and cook for 2 minutes, then turn the cod over and cook for another minute. The fillets should be a nice gold color on both sides. Transfer the fillets to a roasting pan and roast for about 8 minutes; by then the fish should be opaque and cooked through, but still moist.

5. Serve the fish with the bean puree and some of the anchovy dressing spooned over the top.

Henry dollops sour cream over the warm baked beets here instead of mixing them together, which prevents the sour cream from turning purple and murky. It's a gorgeous, fresh-tasting dish.

SWEDISH BAKED BEETS WITH ONIONS, SOUR CREAM & DILL

SERVES 4 TO 6 AS A SIDE DISH

1½ pounds beets
       (try to get small ones)
¼ cup olive oil
Salt and pepper
  2 red onions, cut into
       half-moon-shaped wedges
⅔ cup sour cream
  1 tablespoon coarsely
       chopped fresh dill

The Scandinavians pair the warm sweetness of beets with the saltiness of smoked fish. This dish is lovely with boiled little waxy potatoes and fillets of hot-smoked trout or salmon, or with baked fresh salmon.

1. Preheat the oven to 350°F. Wrap the unpeeled beets in an aluminum foil packet, leaving an opening. Drizzle with half the olive oil, season with salt and pepper, close the packet, and put in a roasting pan. Roast until tender. How long this takes depends on the size of your beets—it could take as long as 1½ hours. Put the onion wedges in a small roasting pan, drizzle with the rest of the olive oil, season with salt and pepper, and roast in the same oven for 20 to 30 minutes. The onions should be tender and slightly singed at the tips.

2. When the beets are tender, peel each one (or leave the skin on if you prefer) and quarter or halve, depending on their size. Season the beets and put on a serving dish with the onions. Daub the sour cream over the vegetables and sprinkle with the dill. Serve hot or at room temperature.

PURE SIMPLE COOKING
Diana Henry

While the eggplants bake, they almost begin to melt; squeezing lemon juice over them brightens their flavor considerably. Use Asian-style or small eggplants, which have the fewest seeds.

TURKISH BAKED EGGPLANT WITH CHILE, FETA & MINT

SERVES 4 AS A STARTER OR SIDE DISH

4 eggplants
Olive oil
Salt and pepper
2 onions, thinly sliced
6 cloves garlic, thinly sliced
2 medium fresh red chiles, halved, seeded, and thinly sliced
Juice of ½ lemon
4 ounces feta cheese, crumbled
¾ cup Greek-style yogurt
A handful of fresh mint leaves, torn
Extra-virgin olive oil

I've never eaten this in Turkey. Somebody described it to me, and I came up with this dish—so I can't claim it as authentic, but who cares? It is a lip-smacking combination of textures and temperatures. Substantial enough to be a main course if you want to serve it that way.

1. Preheat the oven to 400°F. Halve the eggplants lengthwise and then score a diamond pattern into the flesh of each half on the cut surface, being careful not to cut all the way through. Pour about 10 tablespoons olive oil over them and season with salt and pepper. Turn them over to make sure they are well coated. Roast for 40 to 45 minutes.

2. While the eggplants are cooking, sauté the onions in ¼ cup olive oil until soft and golden. Add the garlic and chiles and cook for another 2 minutes, until they are soft as well.

3. When the eggplants are tender, put them on a serving plate, cut side up, and squeeze lemon juice over them. Gently press the cooked flesh down to make a bit of room for the onions. Fill the eggplant cavities with the onions and sprinkle the feta on top.

4. Daub the yogurt over the eggplants and throw on the mint leaves. Drizzle extra-virgin olive oil over the top before serving. You can serve this warm or at room temperature.

Vietnamese cooks traditionally serve each component of a salad separately, but here Henry tosses everything together—chicken, mango, fresh herbs—in a vibrant lime and garlic dressing.

VIETNAMESE GRILLED CHICKEN SALAD

SERVES 6

3   stalks of fresh lemongrass, inner white bulbs only, finely chopped
3   garlic cloves
Kosher salt and freshly ground pepper
5½ tablespoons peanut oil
1   tablespoon Asian fish sauce
1½ teaspoons dark brown sugar
3   boneless chicken breast halves, with skin
3   tablespoons rice vinegar
2   tablespoons fresh lime juice
1½ teaspoons granulated sugar
One 9-ounce head of Bibb lettuce, torn into pieces
2   carrots, cut into matchsticks
1   small firm mango, peeled and cut into matchsticks
½   cucumber, seeded and cut into matchsticks
½   cup bean sprouts
¼   cup small mint leaves
¼   cup small basil leaves

EDITOR'S WINE CHOICE
Juicy, off-dry Riesling:
2009 Clos du Bois

1. In a mini food processor, mince the lemongrass with the garlic and a pinch each of salt and pepper. Add 2½ tablespoons of the peanut oil, 1½ teaspoons of the fish sauce and the brown sugar and process until a paste forms. Set the chicken in a glass baking dish and coat with the paste. Refrigerate for at least 3 hours or overnight.

2. In a small bowl, whisk the remaining 3 tablespoons of peanut oil and 1½ teaspoons of fish sauce with the rice vinegar, lime juice and granulated sugar; season with salt and pepper.

3. Light a grill or preheat a grill pan. Wipe the marinade off the chicken. Season the chicken with salt and pepper and grill over moderate heat until browned and cooked through, about 8 minutes per side. Transfer to a work surface and let rest for 5 minutes.

4. In a large bowl, toss the lettuce with the carrots, mango, cucumber, bean sprouts, mint and basil. Cut the chicken breasts crosswise into ½-inch-thick slices and add to the bowl. Add the dressing and toss to coat. Transfer the salad to plates and serve.

MAKE AHEAD The dressing can be refrigerated for up to 2 days.

DIANA HENRY ONLINE
dianahenry.co.uk

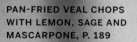

PAN-FRIED VEAL CHOPS
WITH LEMON, SAGE AND
MASCARPONE, P. 189

FALLING CLOUDBERRIES

Tessa Kiros

My mother's name is Sirpa Tuula Kerttu Peiponen. My father's name is George," writes Tessa Kiros, a restaurant cook of Finnish and Greek-Cypriot heritage. Her cookbook is a charming, fascinating blend of home recipes and memories. A chapter called "Monkeys' Weddings" is about South Africa, where she grew up, and features vibrant recipes like shrimp with lemon, peri-peri (a fiery chile), garlic and feta. The Finnish chapter, which gives the book its name, contains a wonderfully fragrant take on traditional cinnamon and cardamom buns. Kiros comes full circle with "Washing Lines and Wishing Wells," referring to Italy, where she is now raising her own family on dishes like Pan-Fried Veal Chops with Lemon, Sage and Mascarpone.

Published by Andrews McMeel, $29.99

To keep shrimp moist, Kiros cooks and serves them with the shells on, so be prepared for a mess with lots of napkins. Neatniks can also try making the recipe with peeled shrimp.

SHRIMP WITH LEMON, PERI-PERI, GARLIC & FETA

SERVES 6 OR MORE

- 4½ pounds large raw shrimp, unpeeled
- 1¾ sticks butter
- 10 garlic cloves, finely chopped
- ¾ cup chopped fresh parsley
- Less than 1 teaspoon peri-peri spice or chile powder (see Author's Note)
- Juice of 4 lemons
- 2⅔ cups crumbled feta cheese

EDITOR'S WINE CHOICE

Bright, lemony Greek white: 2008 Gai'a Notios

AUTHOR'S NOTE

My mother always uses peri-peri, which is a wonderfully flavored full-potency chile that we get in South Africa. Substitute your favorite chile powder or cayenne pepper, using as much as you like. I like a good balance of strong flavors but the chile should not be too overpowering.

This is amazing. Everyone who has tasted this dish loves it and still now I use it for a special occasion dinner—it seems very "celebration." You can clean the shrimp beforehand and keep them covered in a colander in the refrigerator, then you'll only need about 20 minutes before serving. This dish needs very little else—bread, some white rice or couscous, and a large green salad.

Clean the shrimp and cut a slit through the shell down the back from the bottom of the head to the beginning of the tail. Remove the dark vein with the point of a sharp knife. Rinse the shrimp under running water and drain well.

Dot about 5 tablespoons of the butter over the base of a large cast-iron casserole dish. Arrange a single layer of shrimp in the dish and season with salt. Scatter about a third of the garlic and parsley over the top. Sprinkle with a little of the peri-peri.

Dot about half of the remaining butter over the top and arrange another layer of shrimp, scattered with garlic, parsley, and peri-peri. Repeat the layer, finishing up the ingredients. Put the lid on, turn the heat to medium-high, and cook for about 10 minutes, until the shrimp have brightened up a lot and their flesh is white. Add the lemon juice, scatter the feta over the top, and rock the dish from side to side to move the sauce about. Spoon some sauce over the shrimp. Cover the casserole, decrease the heat, and cook for another 10 minutes, or until the feta has just melted, shaking the dish again. Take the dish straight to the table and give everyone a hot finger bowl with lemon juice, to clean their hands afterward.

These Italian-style veal chops cook in a single skillet and have a short ingredient list that belies the complexity of flavor. For a heartier meal, use larger chops; there's plenty of sauce.

PAN-FRIED VEAL CHOPS WITH LEMON, SAGE & MASCARPONE

SERVES 2

1	tablespoon olive oil
1½	tablespoons butter, plus an extra knob
2	veal chops, about $5/8$ inch thick
6	fresh sage leaves, rinsed and dried
1	garlic clove, crushed

Juice of 1 small lemon
⅓ cup mascarpone

EDITOR'S WINE CHOICE

**Soft, cherry-rich Barbera:
2007 Vietti Tre Vigne Barbera d'Asti**

One of my favorite chefs in the world, Angela Dwyer, taught me this recipe. I love lemon; I love veal, sage, and mascarpone; so it is unlikely that I wouldn't love the finished dish. You have to work quickly here so that the butter in the pan doesn't burn and the chops get nicely browned—so have everything ready before you start.

Heat the oil and butter in a large skillet. When it is sizzling, add the chops and cook over high heat, turning over when the underneath is golden. Now add the sage leaves and garlic and season the meat with salt and pepper. Add another knob of butter to the pan to prevent burning. Take out the sage leaves when they are crisp and move the garlic around (or take it out if it starts to look too dark). You might like to turn the meat onto its fat side with a pair of tongs so that the fat browns.

Add the lemon juice to the pan and swirl it around, then add the mascarpone. If the veal is cooked, transfer it to a serving plate while you finish the sauce. If you think the veal needs longer, then leave it in the pan. It should be golden brown on the outside and rosy pink, soft, but cooked through on the inside. Add about 3 tablespoons of water to the pan and scrape up all the bits that are stuck to the bottom. Cook for another couple of minutes, then pour the sauce over the veal and scatter with the crispy sage. Serve immediately with some bread for the sauce.

Instead of using raw egg yolks (which some people shy away from), the nicely pungent Caesar-like dressing here calls for gently cooked eggs. There's lots of leftover dressing for other salads.

CODDLED EGG & ANCHOVY SALAD

SERVES 6

DRESSING

- 2 soft rosemary sprigs, rinsed
- 2 garlic cloves
- 8 oil-packed anchovy fillets, drained and chopped
- 1 heaped tablespoon Dijon mustard
- 2 tablespoons lemon juice
- ½ cup vegetable oil
- ½ cup olive oil
- 2 eggs, at room temperature

SALAD

- 1 fennel bulb, halved and very finely sliced
- ¼ pound (about 4 cups loosely packed) radicchio or trevise leaves, torn into large chunks
- ½ pound (about 10 cups loosely packed) firm inner lettuce leaves
- 2 celery stalks, finely sliced

This is how my friend Jo makes her salad. She is an exceptional cook, full of enthusiasm and fun. She says she also likes this dressing with warm asparagus, broad beans, and peas. I find it also goes well with olives and fresh raw vegetables for dunking into the sauce, or just with a plain steak and some fat fries for dipping. This will make a couple of cups of dressing that you can use as you like.

Bring about 3 cups of salted water to a boil and dunk the rosemary and garlic in the water a few times to soften them slightly. Strip the rosemary leaves off the stem and chop very finely with the garlic. Put in a bowl.

Whisk in the anchovies, mustard, and lemon juice, a few grindings of black pepper, and a little of each of the oils. Whisk well until it all comes together, a bit like mayonnaise.

Meanwhile, lower the eggs into the boiling water and boil for 3 minutes. (To be perfect, all of the white and a fine layer of yolk should be set; the rest of the yolk should be soft.) Rinse under cold water until cool enough to peel. Add to the dressing, whisking to break the eggs into small bits. Add the rest of the oil, whisking continuously until completely combined. Whisk in a teaspoonful of warm water to finish the dressing.

Put all the salad ingredients in a large bowl. Splash the dressing over the top, tossing well so that all the leaves carry a heavy coat of dressing, and serve immediately.

These buns bake into fun, peel-apart layers. The subtle cardamom flavor is wonderful, and because the buns are not too sweet, they're an ideal pastry for any time of day, especially teatime.

CINNAMON & CARDAMOM BUNS

MAKES ABOUT 35 BUNS

BUN DOUGH
- 1 cup lukewarm milk
- ½ cup superfine sugar
- One 1-ounce cake fresh yeast
- 1 egg, lightly beaten
- ¼ pound plus 1 tablespoon butter, softened
- 2 teaspoons ground cardamom
- 1 teaspoon salt
- 5¼ cups all-purpose flour

CINNAMON BUTTER
- 2 teaspoons ground cinnamon
- ¼ cup superfine sugar, plus 1 tablespoon for sprinkling
- 5½ tablespoons butter, softened
- 1 egg, lightly beaten

These gorgeous buns were always a part of my childhood. They are found everywhere in Finland—and probably all over Scandinavia—in tearooms and houses. Everyone makes their own and they freeze beautifully so you can just pull out a few when a craving sets in. Don't be put off when you see that the buns need to rise for a couple of hours. You can get the dough together really quickly and then leave it alone without even a glance. The rolling and cutting can be a little tricky the first time you do it, but the second time will be easy.

Put the milk and sugar in a bowl and crumble in the yeast. Let stand for 10 minutes, or until the yeast begins to activate. Add the egg, butter, cardamom, and salt, and mix in. Add the flour, bit by bit, mixing it in with a wooden spoon until you need to use your hands, and then turn it out onto the work surface to knead. It may seem a little too sticky initially, but will become compact and beautifully soft after about 5 minutes. Put the dough back in the bowl, cover with a clean cloth and then a heavy towel or blanket, and leave in a warm place for about 2 hours, or until it has doubled in size.

To make the cinnamon butter, mix together the cinnamon and sugar. Divide the butter into four portions and set aside.

Put the dough on a floured work surface and divide it into four portions. Begin with one portion, covering the others with a cloth so they don't dry out. Using a rolling pin, roll out a rectangle, roughly about 12 by 10 inches and ⅛ inch thick.

continued on p. 194

Spread one portion of butter over the surface of the dough with a spatula or blunt knife. Sprinkle with about 3 teaspoons of the cinnamon mixture, covering the whole surface with quick shaking movements of your wrists. Roll up to make a long dough sausage. Set aside while you finish rolling out and buttering the rest of the dough, so that you can cut them all together.

Line two large baking sheets with parchment paper, or bake in two batches if you only have one sheet. Line up the dough sausages in front of you and cut them slightly on the diagonal, alternating up and down, so that the slices are fat V shapes, with the point of the V about ¾ inch and the base about 2 inches. Turn them so they are all the right way up, sitting on their fatter bases. Press down on the top of each one with two fingers, until you think you will almost go through to your work surface. Along the sides you will see the cinnamon stripes oozing outward. Put the buns on the baking sheet, leaving space for them to puff and rise while they bake. Brush lightly with beaten egg and sprinkle a little sugar over the top.

Let the buns rise for half an hour and preheat your oven to 350°F. Bake them for about 20 minutes, or until they are golden. Check that they are lightly golden underneath as well before you take them out of the oven. Serve hot, warm, or at room temperature and, when they are cool, keep them in an airtight container so they don't harden.

Kiros has an unusual method for roasting whole chicken: She cooks it breast side down in a shallow pan of water and lemon juice to gently poach the breasts, then turns the bird to brown the skin.

ROASTED LEMON & OREGANO CHICKEN WITH POTATOES

SERVES 4

One 3½-pound chicken
6 Yukon Gold potatoes (about 2 pounds), peeled and quartered lengthwise
3 garlic cloves
2 bay leaves
¼ cup plus 2 tablespoons fresh lemon juice
1 tablespoon dried oregano
Kosher salt and freshly ground pepper
¼ cup plus 2 tablespoons extra-virgin olive oil

EDITOR'S WINE CHOICE

Brisk, elegant Sauvignon Blanc: 2008 Domaine de la Perrière Sancerre

1. Preheat the oven to 325°F. Set the chicken in a roasting pan and scatter the potatoes, garlic and bay leaves around it. Drizzle the lemon juice all over the chicken and potatoes, making sure to get some inside the chicken. Season with the oregano and salt and pepper. Turn the chicken breast side down and drizzle with the olive oil. Pour ½ cup of water into the pan. Roast the chicken for about 1½ hours, until golden.

2. Gently turn the chicken breast side up and turn the potatoes in the juices. Roast the chicken for about 1 hour longer, until golden brown and cooked through. Transfer the chicken to a work surface and let rest for 10 minutes. Discard the bay leaves. Carve the chicken and serve with the potatoes, garlic and pan juices.

TESSA KIROS ONLINE
tessakiros.com

TUNISIAN CARROT
SALAD, P. 198

MEDITERRANEAN HOT AND SPICY

Aglaia Kremezi

The cookbook category is packed with Mediterranean titles—fast, slow, vegetarian, diet. Now Aglaia Kremezi, the award-winning author of *The Foods of Greece,* has written a book for Mediterranean chile heads. She explores fiery ingredients like burning-hot harissa chile paste from Tunisia, which she uses to spice up her mashed-carrot salad. Chiles are not the only source of heat in these dishes. Sometimes black pepper, cinnamon or ginger provides the kick. Kremezi may shock traditionalists; she reinvents the normally delicate Spanish almond and garlic soup called *ajo blanco* with the inspired, if unorthodox, addition of ginger. In a charming defense of her soup, she writes, "I'm sure that in its medieval form it was much spicier."

Published by Broadway Books, $19.95

This is a fabulous way to cook carrots. Kremezi mashes them with a few strong-flavored ingredients: garlic, lemon, caraway, cilantro and harissa, Tunisia's famous chile paste.

TUNISIAN CARROT SALAD

MAKES 4 SERVINGS AS AN APPETIZER

- 1 pound carrots
- 2 garlic cloves, minced, or 1 teaspoon roasted garlic paste
- 2 to 3 tablespoons fresh lemon juice
- ½ to 1 teaspoon harissa or any hot pepper paste
- 1½ teaspoons ground caraway seeds, preferably freshly ground
- ½ cup chopped fresh cilantro leaves
- 3 to 4 tablespoons olive oil
- Sea salt
- A few kalamata olives for garnish
- ½ cup diced feta cheese (optional)
- 1 or 2 Lemon Slices in Spicy Olive Oil (optional; recipe follows)

The mashed vegetable salads of North Africa have a complex, deep flavor that belies how easy they are to make.

Peel the carrots, chop coarsely, and transfer to a saucepan. Cover the carrots with cold water and bring to a boil. Reduce the heat to low, and simmer the carrots until tender, about 20 minutes. Drain, then mash with a fork or pass through a food mill fitted with the medium disk into a large bowl. Mix in the garlic, 2 tablespoons of the lemon juice, the harissa, the caraway, and the cilantro. Stir in the olive oil and salt to taste. Taste and add lemon, salt, or harissa as needed. Let cool and refrigerate for at least 3 hours or overnight.

Just before serving, decorate with olives and feta and chopped lemon slices if you like.

LEMON SLICES IN SPICY OLIVE OIL

Wash and dry the lemons thoroughly. Cut them into ⅛-inch-thick slices and lay one layer in a stainless-steel colander. Sprinkle the lemon slices with plenty of salt and repeat, making more layers until you have used all the lemons and salt. Set aside to drain for 24 hours.

Press the lemon slices carefully with paper towels to extract most of the juice, then pack the slices in a 1-pint jar, adding the peperoncini between the slices. Completely cover the lemon slices with olive oil. Close the jar. The lemon slices will keep in the refrigerator for 3 to 6 months.

MAKES 2 CUPS

- 3 or 4 lemons, preferably organic
- 4 to 6 tablespoons sea salt
- 2 to 3 dried peperoncini (or any other chile), cut in half lengthwise with scissors but still attached to the stem
- About 1 cup olive oil

Instead of cooking bulgur, Kremezi simply soaks it in water for 30 minutes. Then, to add depth of flavor, she tosses the bulgur with four kinds of nuts and a tangy dressing.

SPICY BULGUR WITH NUTS & TOMATO PASTE DRESSING

MAKES 8 TO 10 SERVINGS AS AN APPETIZER

2⅔ cups coarse bulgur, soaked in cold water for 20 to 30 minutes, or until tender
¾ cup extra-virgin olive oil
3 tablespoons pomegranate molasses, or juice of 1 lemon, or more to taste
¼ cup plus 2 tablespoons tomato paste
2 teaspoons ground cumin
2 tablespoons ground coriander seeds
½ to 1 teaspoon ground allspice
½ to 1 teaspoon cayenne, or 1 to 3 teaspoons Aleppo or Maraş pepper, or a pinch of hot red pepper flakes, to taste
Sea salt
1 cup coarsely ground walnuts
1 cup coarsely ground toasted hazelnuts
½ cup coarsely ground toasted salted almonds
½ cup toasted pine nuts
⅔ cup chopped fresh cilantro or flat-leaf parsley
8 to 10 medium romaine lettuce leaves (optional)

TOPPINGS (OPTIONAL)
1 small sweet onion, chopped
⅓ cup sliced or chopped fresh or pickled red or green chiles

This hearty salad became our standard picnic dish. We always make it the night before for our lunch on the beach with friends. Grilled fish or lamb chops on our small portable BBQ is the main dish, but everybody raves about the bulgur salad. The recipe is based on Bazargan, *a Syrian-Jewish salad that Claudia Roden included in* A Book of Middle Eastern Food. *I first tasted it many years ago, during a food conference, and I was immediately fascinated by this earthy, fragrant, and crunchy sweet-and-sour mixture.*

Drain the bulgur well in a strainer lined with cheesecloth and pat with paper towels to extract all the water.

In a bowl, whisk together the olive oil, pomegranate molasses, tomato paste, and spices, adding salt sparingly.

In a large bowl, mix the bulgur with the nuts and add the cilantro. Pour the oil mixture over the bulgur mixture and toss well. Cover and refrigerate for at least 3 hours, preferably overnight. Taste and adjust the seasoning just before serving, preferably at room temperature. If you are using the toppings, toss half with the bulgur at the last minute. Spoon onto lettuce leaves if you like or serve in a bowl, sprinkling with the rest of the toppings. The bulgur salad keeps well in the refrigerator for about 4 days.

Variation

Instead of soaking the bulgur in water, you can place the grain in a bowl and pour 1 quart warm tomato juice over it. Let sit for 15 to 20 minutes to absorb the juice, toss well, and continue adding the rest of the ingredients as directed.

Meaty seafood like swordfish can sometimes dry out; simmering the steaks in a sweet-tangy tomato-chile sauce keeps them moist.

SWORDFISH WITH WINE, TOMATO, CHILE & CAPERS

MAKES 4 SERVINGS

Olive oil
2   cups chopped onion
Sea salt
½   cup dry white wine
2   tablespoons red wine vinegar, or more to taste
1 to 3 dried peperoncini or chiles de árbol, thinly sliced with scissors, to taste
2   cups chopped or grated ripe fresh tomato or good-quality canned tomatoes with their juice
¼   cup capers, preferably salt-packed, rinsed well and drained
½ to 1 teaspoon honey or sugar, to taste
4   swordfish or tuna steaks, 6 to 7 ounces each
½   teaspoon freshly ground black pepper, mixed with 1 teaspoon ground coriander seeds
2   tablespoons chopped fresh flat-leaf parsley

EDITOR'S WINE CHOICE

Robust, zesty Italian white:
2008 Argiolas Costamolino
Vermentino

This Calabrian-inspired recipe is easy and fresh tasting. Serve with crusty bread for sopping up the wonderful juices. The fish steaks and sauce can also be served on top of freshly cooked spaghetti or linguine tossed with olive oil.

Heat 3 to 4 tablespoons olive oil in a large skillet over medium-high heat. Add the onion, sprinkle with salt, and sauté, stirring often, until soft and light golden, about 10 minutes. Add the wine, vinegar, and peperoncini and toss for 30 seconds. Pour in the tomatoes and cook for 5 minutes. Add the capers and ½ teaspoon honey and cook for another 8 to 10 minutes, until the sauce thickens. Taste and adjust the flavor with more chile, vinegar, or honey. It should be quite intense—more or less sour, according to your taste. Transfer the sauce to a bowl and wipe the skillet with paper towels.

Heat 3 tablespoons olive oil in the skillet over medium-high heat. Sprinkle the fish steaks with salt and rub with the pepper-coriander mixture. Add to the hot skillet and sauté for 2 to 3 minutes on each side, until firm but still almost raw in the center. Add the sauce, bring to a boil, and cook for about 5 minutes, or until the fish is firm and just cooked through. Let the fish and sauce cool for 15 minutes or longer, then sprinkle with parsley and serve warm or at room temperature.

Because its ingredients are chopped, then blended with yogurt, this salad is really more like a dip. Creamy and tart, it's perfect on toasts.

YOGURT, SPINACH & PARSLEY SALAD WITH WALNUTS (BORANI)

MAKES ABOUT 3 CUPS

1½   pounds spinach leaves, coarsely chopped
1   cup chopped fresh flat-leaf parsley
½   cup chopped fresh cilantro
3   cups Greek yogurt, preferably sheep's milk
2 or 3 garlic cloves, minced, to taste
1 to 3 jalapeño chiles, finely chopped, to taste
Sea salt and freshly ground black pepper
½   cup coarsely chopped walnuts

As is the case with some Mediterranean dishes, the term borani *means different things in the countries of the region. Spinach, eggplant, zucchini, or any other vegetable mixed with yogurt is the most common borani, both in the Middle East and in the Balkans. The dish originates in Persia (Iran), and its name is believed to derive from a Persian queen who was fond of yogurt. But in the Gaziantep, in Turkish Anatolia, borani is a dish that combines black-eyed peas, ground meat, and chard. The recipe that follows mixes both cooked spinach and fresh parsley and cilantro and is my adaptation of an Armenian dish. As an alternative to the traditional pita bread, I prefer to spread borani on toasted whole wheat or multigrain bread rubbed with a cut clove of garlic. Borani can also be a side dish, accompanying poached or grilled fish or chicken.*

Wash the spinach in a saucepan and place it over high heat. Cover and steam it until wilted in the water that clings to the leaves, 2 to 3 minutes. Toss once or twice while cooking and be careful not to let it burn. Remove the spinach from the heat, turn it into a colander, and let it cool and drain. Press with your hands to remove as much liquid as possible. Finely chop the spinach and transfer to a bowl.

Add the parsley, cilantro, yogurt, garlic, and chiles, stirring well. Add a little salt, taste, and add more if necessary along with a little black pepper. Cover and refrigerate for at least 3 hours or overnight.

Spread on toasts, sprinkle with walnuts, and serve as an appetizer or transfer to a serving dish and sprinkle with walnuts.

BEST OF THE BEST EXCLUSIVE

This rustic Greek and Balkan pie cooks until it's crisp outside, moist inside. Serve it as finger food, a starter or a vegetarian main course.

CRUSTLESS ZUCCHINI PIE

MAKES 8 FIRST-COURSE SERVINGS

- 2 pounds zucchini, coarsely grated (about 8 packed cups)
- 2 teaspoons kosher salt
- ⅓ cup plus 1½ teaspoons extra-virgin olive oil
- ½ cup yellow cornmeal
- ½ medium yellow onion, finely chopped
- 4 ounces feta cheese, crumbled (about ¾ cup)
- ¼ cup packed mint leaves, finely chopped
- 2 large eggs, lightly beaten
- ¼ teaspoon freshly ground pepper
- 3 tablespoons dry bread crumbs

EDITOR'S WINE CHOICE

Bright, floral Argentinean white: 2009 Crios de Susana Balbo Torrontés

1. In a strainer set over a bowl, toss the zucchini with the salt. Let drain for 30 minutes.

2. Preheat the oven to 400°F. Squeeze the zucchini dry and transfer to a bowl. Add ⅓ cup of the olive oil and the cornmeal, onion, feta, mint, eggs and pepper and mix until evenly blended. Pat the zucchini mixture into a 9-by-13-inch glass baking dish. Sprinkle the bread crumbs over the top and drizzle with the remaining 1½ teaspoons of olive oil.

3. Bake the zucchini pie for 10 minutes. Reduce the oven temperature to 375°F and continue to bake for about 30 minutes, until the top and edges are golden brown. Remove from the oven and let stand for 15 minutes before serving. Cut the pie into 8 squares and serve warm or at room temperature.

SERVE WITH A green salad.

AGLAIA KREMEZI ONLINE
aglaiakremezi.com

STRAW AND HAY AL FORNO, P. 208

MEDITERRANEAN CLAY POT COOKING

Paula Wolfert

Paula Wolfert is the definitive expert on Mediterranean food—a legend, really—so when she writes, "Most food tastes better cooked in clay," it's compelling. In the course of researching seven cookbooks over the past 35 years, including her first, the groundbreaking *Couscous and Other Good Food from Morocco*, Wolfert discovered that earthenware and stoneware impart an earthy flavor to food. This book introduces readers to clay pots from around the Mediterranean and to recipes like France's chicken with red wine vinegar, which is especially good when cooked in a Spanish cazuela (a glazed earthenware vessel). And while a dome-lidded tagine isn't required to prepare her Moroccan lamb and spinach stew—a cast-iron casserole will do—readers will want to try it.

Published by John Wiley & Sons, $34.95

This is the kind of recipe that will make you want to rush out and buy a clay pot. The creamy, tangy, intensely flavorful chicken thighs, finished with a small amount of crème fraîche, are that good.

CHICKEN WITH RED WINE VINEGAR, TOMATO & SHALLOTS

SERVES 4 TO 6

8 large chicken thighs (about 3½ pounds), preferably organic

Salt and freshly ground black pepper

¾ cup plus 2 tablespoons red wine vinegar, preferably homemade

1 tablespoon strong chicken stock or glace de poulet diluted in ½ cup water or ½ cup rich chicken stock

1 tablespoon honey

¼ cup thick tomato sauce or 1 tablespoon tomato paste

2 tablespoons unsalted butter

¾ cup thinly sliced shallot

2 tablespoons thinly sliced garlic

¾ cup dry white wine, such as Viognier, at room temperature

2 tablespoons crème fraîche

3 tablespoons chopped fresh tarragon

PREFERRED CLAY POT

A 10- or 11-inch straight-sided flameware skillet or a Spanish cazuela

If using an electric or ceramic stovetop, be sure to use a heat diffuser with the clay pot.

EDITOR'S WINE CHOICE

Blackberry-scented, spicy Côtes du Rhône: 2006 Domaine de Monpertuis Vignoble de la Ramière

I think of this popular French dish as "comfort" food. All the flavors are familiar yet greatly magnified by steady slow cooking. Something wondrous emerges as vinegar, rich tomato sauce, shallot, garlic, and a touch of honey slowly meld together in a clay pot. Long cooking of the vinegar softens acidity while deepening flavor, with the result that the sauce comes out perfectly balanced and never overwhelms the chicken.

1. Rinse the chicken thighs; pat dry and trim away all excess fat. Season the chicken with salt and pepper. Let stand at room temperature while you prepare the sauce.

2. In a medium nonreactive saucepan, combine the vinegar, chicken stock, honey, and tomato sauce. Boil until reduced to ¾ cup. Remove from the heat and keep warm.

3. Set the flameware skillet over medium-low heat. Add the butter; when foaming, slowly raise the heat to medium. Add half the pieces of chicken; brown well on all sides, 6 to 8 minutes. Transfer to a side dish and repeat with the remaining chicken.

4. Add the shallot and garlic to the pan; cook slowly until soft, about 5 minutes. Pour the warm sauce into the pan and slowly bring to a boil. Return the chicken thighs to the skillet, skin side up. Slowly pour in the wine. Season with 2 pinches of salt and 1 pinch of pepper. Cover, raise the heat to medium, and simmer until the chicken is tender, about 20 minutes. Remove the chicken, cover with foil, and let rest while you finish the sauce.

5. Stir the crème fraîche into the skillet and boil for a few minutes. Season with salt and pepper to taste. Return the chicken to the pot and top with the chopped tarragon.

MEDITERRANEAN CLAY POT COOKING
Paula Wolfert

Straw and Hay is an Italian classic combining green and white pasta. Wolfert prefers using a Spanish cazuela for this indulgent spring recipe, but a glass or ceramic baking dish works, too.

STRAW & HAY AL FORNO

SERVES 2 TO 3

    3 baby artichokes
       (4 to 5 ounces total)
2 to 2½ ounces fresh wild mushrooms,
       preferably small chanterelles
       or trumpet mushrooms
    2 tablespoons extra-virgin olive oil
Salt and freshly ground black pepper
    2 tablespoons finely chopped
       white onion
    2 garlic cloves, mashed
    2 ounces flavorful cooked ham,
       cut into ½-inch dice
    ¾ cup heavy cream
    ¾ cup milk
    ⅛ teaspoon freshly grated nutmeg
    ⅓ cup plus 2 tablespoons freshly
       grated Parmigiano-Reggiano
       cheese
    4 ounces dried egg noodles—
       half green spinach tagliatelle
       and half plain

PREFERRED CLAY POT
A shallow 10-inch Spanish cazuela
    or a straight-sided flameware or
    La Chamba skillet
If using an electric or ceramic stovetop,
    be sure to use a heat diffuser
    with the clay pot.

The Napa Valley restaurant Bistro Don Giovanni is just twenty minutes by car from my home. Here Chef Scott Warner produces marvelous food for vintners and tourists alike, including great pizzas and pasta dishes baked in his wood-fired ovens. When I asked him for a good clay pot–driven recipe for this book, he suggested this rich version of Straw and Hay. Scott boils his green and white pasta, tosses it with baby artichokes, wild mushrooms, ham, and just enough cream and cheese to create an evenly balanced dish. Then he finishes it off in his wood-fired oven, baking the pasta in the gratin dish in which it is served at table.

Not having a wood-fired oven, I've tried this dish in my ordinary oven and also in my double clay–slabbed oven. It worked well both ways. Use a Spanish cazuela to cook the vegetables; then toss in the pasta, cream, and cheese and bake until bubbly.

You can easily find the half plain egg, half spinach pasta shaped into nests or in long strips packaged together in good food shops. Note that Steps 1 and 2 can be done several hours in advance.

1. Wash the artichokes; trim the stems and remove the tough outer leaves. Boil or microwave in salted water until just tender, about 10 minutes. Immediately drain, cool, and gently press out excess moisture. Wrap in paper towels and set aside.

2. To clean the mushrooms, simply toss them in a deep sieve and shake vigorously to release any surface dirt. Trim the ends and use a water spray to rinse them quickly; drain and blot dry. Coat the bottom of the cazuela with 1 tablespoon of the olive oil and set it over low heat. When the oil is warm, add the mushrooms. Cover with a lid or foil, and steam for 3 to 4 minutes. Then uncover, raise the heat to medium, and sauté until the mushrooms express all their moisture and begin to caramelize. Transfer the mushrooms to a side dish. Set the hot cazuela aside on a wooden surface or folded kitchen towel to prevent cracking; do not wash it.

3. About 30 minutes before serving, preheat the oven to 400°F. Gently press down on each cooked artichoke and thinly slice lengthwise. Season lightly with salt and pepper.

4. Add another tablespoon of olive oil to the cazuela and set it over medium heat. Add the onion and cook until it is soft and lightly caramelized, 10 minutes. Add the garlic, ham, artichokes, and cooked mushrooms. Continue to cook until the garlic is lightly toasted, about 3 to 5 minutes.

5. In a small conventional saucepan, heat the cream and milk until hot. Season with the nutmeg and salt and pepper to taste. Pour the seasoned milk and cream into the cazuela and bring to a boil. Turn off the heat, stir in ⅓ cup of the cheese, and let the sauce stand until you're ready to add the pasta.

6. In a large conventional pot of boiling salted water, cook the pasta until just tender, 9 to 10 minutes. Meanwhile, if necessary, reheat the sauce in the cazuela until hot. Drain the pasta and add to the cazuela, stirring to coat with the sauce. Scatter the remaining 2 tablespoons cheese on top.

7. Transfer the cazuela to the top third of the oven. Bake until the top is lightly browned and the dish is bubbling, 15 to 20 minutes. Serve at once.

The eggplant and tomatoes in this tian (a French dish prepared in an earthenware casserole) are incredibly tasty. That's because Wolfert salts the vegetables to concentrate the flavor.

TIAN OF EGGPLANT, TOMATO & FRESH CHEESE

SERVES 4 TO 5

1¼ pounds long, slender eggplants
Coarse salt
  6 small ripe tomatoes
    (about 1½ pounds)
  ½ cup soft cheese, such as ricotta
    or fresh goat cheese, at room
    temperature
1½ tablespoons all-purpose flour
  ⅓ cup milk
  1 egg
  ½ teaspoon freshly ground
    black pepper
  ¼ teaspoon freshly grated nutmeg
  3 tablespoons extra-virgin olive oil
  1 bay leaf
  2 fresh thyme sprigs
  ¼ cup chopped fresh flat-leaf parsley
  ½ cup chopped spring bulb onion,
    green or bunching onion,
    or fat scallions
  2 garlic cloves, peeled and bruised
1½ ounces Parmigiano-Reggiano
    cheese, grated (⅓ cup)
  2 pinches of sugar

PREFERRED CLAY POT
A 9- or 10-inch round earthenware
    baking dish or pie dish

SUGGESTED CLAY ENVIRONMENT
Double slabs of pizza stones or food-safe
    quarry tiles set on the upper and
    lower oven racks

Here is a personal favorite, a tian of ripe summer vegetables at their peak—layers of small heirloom tomatoes, sweet bulb onions, thin-skinned eggplant, and fresh salty cheese such as ricotta or chèvre. I like to prepare this tian in the morning and serve it no sooner than 6 hours after it has emerged from the oven, allowing time for the flavors to meld. It should be left at room temperature; refrigeration diminishes the taste.

My method of setting the tian in a preheated clay-lined oven and then, at the appropriate time, turning the oven off and allowing the tian to set for an additional thirty minutes in the receding heat simulates the way food cooks in a traditional wood-burning oven. That is, first the food is cooked in the hottest part over the wood fire; then the tian is moved to the coolest part of the oven to finish the development of its topping.

1. Trim and peel the eggplants. Cut lengthwise into slices about ½ inch thick. Sprinkle both sides with salt and drain in a colander for 30 minutes. Rinse the eggplant slices and pat dry.

2. Use a serrated swivel-bladed vegetable peeler to skin the tomatoes or dip them briefly in a pot of boiling water and slip off the skins. Slice the tomatoes and spread them out on paper towels. Dust lightly with coarse salt.

3. In a mixing bowl, mash the soft cheese with the flour and milk until smooth. Beat in the egg. Season with ½ teaspoon salt, the pepper, and the nutmeg. Set the cheese mixture aside.

continued on p. 212

4. Heat 1 tablespoon of the olive oil in a medium conventional skillet. Add the bay leaf, thyme, parsley, spring bulb onion, and one of the garlic cloves. Cook over medium-low heat until the onion is soft and golden, about 10 minutes. Remove from the heat and discard the bay leaf.

5. Preheat the oven to 400°F. Set a ridged grill pan over medium-high heat; lightly brush with olive oil. When the pan is hot, grill the eggplant, in batches as necessary, turning once, until lightly browned, about 2 minutes on each side.

6. Rub the earthenware baking dish with the second garlic clove and brush with oil. Layer about half of the eggplant slices over the bottom. Combine the onion and cheese mixture and spread on top. Cover with a layer of half of the tomatoes. Add another layer of eggplant slices, sprinkle with the Parmigiano-Reggiano cheese, and top with the remaining tomato slices. Sprinkle the sugar and remaining oil on top and bake for 1 hour.

7. Turn off the heat and leave the tian in the oven for another 45 to 60 minutes, or until the tomatoes acquire a lovely charred edge but remain shiny on top. Serve directly from the dish at room temperature. Do not refrigerate.

A tagine is both a Moroccan stew and the pot it's cooked in. This one features gently spiced lamb cooked under a blanket of freshly steamed spinach flavored with olives and preserved lemon.

LAMB TAGINE SMOTHERED IN BABY SPINACH

SERVES 4

- 12 cilantro sprigs
- 12 flat-leaf parsley sprigs
- 3 tablespoons extra-virgin olive oil
- ½ red onion, coarsely grated
- 1½ pounds boneless lamb shoulder, cut into 1½-inch pieces
- ½ teaspoon ground ginger
- ½ teaspoon freshly ground white pepper
- ½ teaspoon turmeric
- ¼ teaspoon ground cumin
- ¼ teaspoon cinnamon
- Pinch of freshly grated nutmeg
- ½ cup water
- Kosher salt
- 1 pound baby spinach
- 12 green olives, such as Picholine, pitted and quartered
- ¼ preserved lemon rind, thinly sliced

EDITOR'S WINE CHOICE

Concentrated, peppery Cabernet Franc: 2008 Domaine Lavigne Saumur-Champigny

1. Using butchers' twine, tie the cilantro and parsley sprigs into a bundle. In a 2-quart tagine, heat 2 tablespoons of the olive oil. Add the onion and cook over moderately low heat until softened, about 10 minutes. Add the lamb and cook over moderately high heat until lightly browned in spots, about 6 minutes. Add the herb bundle, ginger, white pepper, turmeric, cumin, cinnamon, nutmeg, water and ½ teaspoon salt. Cover and cook over low heat until the lamb is tender, about 2½ hours.

2. Meanwhile, put the spinach in a large glass bowl, cover with plastic wrap and microwave at high power until wilted, about 3 minutes. Drain any excess water from the spinach. Toss the spinach with the remaining 1 tablespoon of olive oil and season with salt.

3. Discard the herb bundle from the tagine and skim off any excess fat. Spoon the spinach over the lamb, sprinkle with the olives and preserved lemon and serve.

SERVE WITH Warm flatbread.

NOTE If you don't own a tagine, use a 2-quart enameled cast-iron casserole instead.

MAKE AHEAD The lamb stew can be refrigerated for up to 2 days. Reheat and top with the spinach before serving.

PAULA WOLFERT ONLINE

paula-wolfert.com

f Paula Wolfert

t @soumak

STIR-FRIED "BEEF"
WITH BROCCOLI, P. 218

MASTERING THE ART OF CHINESE COOKING

Eileen Yin-Fei Lo

Revered author and Chinese-cooking instructor Eileen Yin-Fei Lo has taught everything from basic to advanced cooking classes, and in this comprehensive tome she shares the full curriculum. She begins in Chinatown, the basis for a detailed glossary of ingredients and an overview of such fundamental techniques as the simple but usually mangled stir-fry. This yields recipes like Clams Stir-Fried with Black Beans that taste better than most restaurant versions. Short sections on regional cuisines, lesser-known recipes (yes, there are wheat breads in China, like Beijing baked bread, brushed with scallion oil) and special categories like dim sum and banquets follow. At the end of this tour de force, Lo concludes: "You are now ready to cook."

Published by Chronicle Books, $50

Though simple, this fried rice packs a ton of flavor from ginger, garlic, sweet shallots and eggs. To make it an even more substantial meal, add shrimp, chicken or roasted pork.

A SIMPLE FRIED RICE

MAKES 6 SERVINGS

SAUCE
- 2 tablespoons oyster sauce
- 2 tablespoons light soy sauce
- 1 tablespoon Shaoxing wine
- 1 teaspoon sugar
- ¼ teaspoon of salt

Pinch of white pepper

- 5 cups cooked rice, at room temperature
- 1 cup fresh or frozen green peas
- 2 cups water, if using fresh peas
- 5 extra-large eggs
- 4½ tablespoons peanut oil
- ½ teaspoon salt

Pinch of white pepper

- 2 teaspoons minced ginger
- 2 teaspoons minced garlic
- ½ cup ¼-inch-dice shallots

Here is one of my time-honored family recipes, an everyday dish of fried rice with green peas. This is the most basic use for cooked, or leftover, rice. It traditionally relies on fresh peas for its flavor, though nowadays flash-frozen peas are nearly as good as fresh. The peas, together with the seasoning mix, give an elegance to this simplest of dishes, commonly found in nearly every home, rural or urban.

This recipe illustrates how important it is to have all of the ingredients for a stir-fry at hand before you begin cooking so the frying can proceed without interruption. All of the ingredients for this dish can be prepared up to 3 hours in advance of cooking.

1. To make the sauce: In a small bowl, mix together all of the ingredients and reserve.

2. Place the cooked rice in a bowl. Using your hands, break up any lumps and reserve.

3. If using fresh peas, pour the water into a small pot and bring to a boil over high heat. Add the peas and boil for 1 to 2 minutes, or until they are tender. Drain and reserve. If using frozen peas, allow them to thaw, then drain well and reserve.

4. In a bowl, beat the eggs with 1 tablespoon of the peanut oil, ¼ teaspoon of the salt, and the white pepper.

5. Heat a wok over high heat for 30 seconds. Add 2 tablespoons of the peanut oil and, using a spatula, coat the wok with the oil. When a wisp of white smoke appears, add the beaten eggs and scramble with the spatula for about 1½ minutes, or until medium-firm. Turn off the heat and transfer to a plate. Cut into small, coarse pieces, and reserve.

6. Wash and dry the wok and spatula. Heat the wok over high heat for 20 seconds. Add the remaining 1½ tablespoons peanut oil and, using the spatula, coat the wok with the oil. When a wisp of white smoke appears, add the ginger and stir briefly. Then add the garlic and stir briefly. Add the shallots and the remaining ¼ teaspoon salt, lower the heat to medium, and cook for 2 minutes, or until the shallots are translucent. Add the peas, raise the heat to high, and stir and cook for 2 minutes, or until very hot. Add the rice, stir to mix, then lower the heat to medium, and stir and mix for 3 minutes, or until the rice is very hot.

7. Raise the heat to high, stir the sauce, and drizzle it over the rice. Stir constantly for about 2 minutes, or until the rice is evenly coated with the sauce. Add the eggs and stir and mix for about 2 minutes, or until all of the ingredients are blended.

8. Turn off the heat, transfer to a heated dish, and serve.

The sauce that lightly coats the "beef" (actually, tofu) and broccoli in this vegetarian recipe is a vast improvement on the thick, gloppy kind offered by too many Chinese restaurants in the United States.

STIR-FRIED "BEEF" WITH BROCCOLI

MAKES 4 TO 6 SERVINGS

SAUCE

- 2 tablespoons oyster sauce
- 2 teaspoons dark soy sauce
- 2 teaspoons Shaoxing wine
- ½ teaspoon sesame oil
- 1¼ teaspoons sugar
- 1 tablespoon cornstarch
- Pinch of white pepper
- ½ cup vegetable stock

- 3 heads broccoli, 1 pound each
- 2 quarts water
- ½-inch-thick slice ginger, peeled and lightly smashed
- 1 tablespoon salt
- 1 teaspoon baking soda (optional)

- 3 tablespoons peanut oil
- 2 teaspoons minced garlic
- 6 seasoned bean curd cakes (8 ounces), cut into ⅛-inch-thick slices
- ¼ teaspoon salt
- 2 tablespoons minced ginger

Here, seasoned bean curd stands in for beef. Many of the vegetarian versions of familiar dishes that use bean curd, both fresh and preserved, are found in the kitchens of the Taoist monastery of Ching Chung Koon, in Hong Kong's New Territories. It is where I first observed them being prepared and later cooked them.

1. To make the sauce, in a small bowl, mix together all of the ingredients and reserve.

2. To water-blanch the broccoli, first trim the broccoli heads into florets. You should have about 1 pound florets. In a pot, bring the water to a boil over high heat. Add the ginger, salt, and baking soda (if using). When the water returns to a boil, add the broccoli and blanch for 10 seconds, then turn off the heat. The broccoli will turn bright green immediately on being immersed in the water. The extra seconds will tenderize the florets. Run cold water into the pot, then drain off the water. Run cold water into the pot again, then drain the broccoli in a strainer over a bowl and reserve. Discard the ginger.

3. Heat a wok over high heat for 30 seconds. Add 1½ tablespoons of the peanut oil and, using a spatula, coat the wok with the oil. When a wisp of white smoke appears, add the garlic and stir briefly until the garlic turns light brown. Add the bean curd slices and stir-fry for 2 minutes, or until thoroughly mixed with the garlic. Turn off the heat, transfer to a small dish, and reserve.

4. Turn on the heat to high under the wok. Add the remaining 1½ tablespoons peanut oil, the salt, and ginger and stir for 45 seconds, or until very hot. Add the reserved broccoli and stir-fry for 2 minutes, or until the broccoli is well coated with the ginger and oil. Add the reserved bean curd and stir-fry for 1½ minutes, or until all of the ingredients are well mixed and very hot. Make a well in the center of the mixture, stir the sauce, and pour it into the well. Stir and mix for about 2 minutes, or until the sauce thickens and bubbles.

5. Turn off the heat, transfer to a heated plate, and serve.

Fermented black beans add a salty, funky depth to this authentic, briny stir-fry; look for them at Asian markets. If you can't find mung bean starch, you can substitute cornstarch instead.

CLAMS STIR-FRIED WITH BLACK BEANS

MAKES 4 SERVINGS

2	quarts water
30	medium-size clams, scrubbed with a stiff brush to remove sand and grit

SAUCE

⅔	cup chicken stock
1½	tablespoons oyster sauce
1½	teaspoons dark soy sauce
1	teaspoon sesame oil
1	tablespoon mung bean starch
1	teaspoon sugar

Pinch of white pepper

3	tablespoons peanut oil
2	tablespoons peeled and shredded ginger
2	tablespoons julienned garlic
3	tablespoons fermented black beans, rinsed twice and well drained
1	tablespoon thinly sliced fresh coriander leaves
1	tablespoon thinly sliced green scallion tops

EDITOR'S WINE CHOICE

**Cherry-rich, medium-bodied Pinot Noir:
2009 Cono Sur Bicycle**

This is a familiar Cantonese classic that has survived its trip to the West relatively unscathed. Often, however, foolish shortcuts are taken. For example, the clams and sauce are cooked separately and the sauce is simply poured over them. Of course, this doesn't flavor the clams, making the method unacceptable. A fine dish like this, no matter how familiar, should be cooked properly, according to tradition.

1. Pour the water into a wok and bring to a boil over high heat. Add the clams and allow the water to return to a boil. This will take 4 to 5 minutes. The clams will begin to open. Move them about with a spatula to help the process along. As they open, remove them to a waiting dish, to prevent them from becoming tough. Continue until all of the clams have opened (discard any that do not open). Set the clams aside. Discard the water and wash and dry the wok and spatula and reserve.

2. To make the sauce: In a small bowl, mix together all of the ingredients and reserve.

3. Heat the wok over high heat for 40 seconds. Add the peanut oil and, using the spatula, coat the wok with the oil. When a wisp of white smoke appears, add the ginger, garlic, and black beans and stir to mix well for about 1 minute, or until the garlic and black beans release their fragrance. Add the clams and stir to mix for 2 minutes. Make a well in the center of the clams, stir the sauce, and pour it into the well. Stir constantly for about 2 minutes, or until the sauce thickens and the clams are thoroughly coated with the sauce.

4. Turn off the heat and transfer to a heated dish. Sprinkle with the coriander and scallion and serve.

For anyone intimidated by cooking duck, Lo's method is reassuring. She bakes the breasts skin side down in a very hot oven to render the fat and crisp the skin, then simply turns them over to finish cooking.

BAKED DUCK BREASTS

MAKES 4 SERVINGS

MARINADE
- 2 tablespoons oyster sauce
- 1½ tablespoons Shaoxing wine
- 1 tablespoon sesame oil
- 4 teaspoons bean sauce
- 2 teaspoons double dark soy sauce
- 2 teaspoons light soy sauce
- 1½ teaspoons peeled and minced ginger
- 1 tablespoon sugar
- ¾ teaspoon five-spice powder
- ½ teaspoon salt
- Pinch of white pepper

- 2 boneless, skin-on whole duck breasts, 1½ pounds total

EDITOR'S WINE CHOICE

Spicy, red berry–scented Syrah: 2007 Cuvaison Carneros

AUTHOR'S NOTE

Once cooked, the breasts can be eaten as they are or saved for future use. They have a pleasantly faint sweetness, which makes the meat a good addition to stir-fries and other recipes. I recommend accompanying them with stir-fried bok choy.

This is an alternative to roasting a whole duck. The technique is simple and quick.

1. To make the marinade: In a small bowl, mix together all of the ingredients and reserve.

2. Rinse the duck breasts under cold running water and dry well with paper towels. Cut each breast in half lengthwise to create 4 pieces total. Using a sharp knife, score the skin, without piercing the meat, in a crisscross pattern. Place the breast pieces, skin side up, in a small roasting pan lined with heavy-duty aluminum foil. Pour the marinade over the breasts and rub in well. Refrigerate for 2 hours, turning them over after 1 hour.

3. About 20 minutes before the breasts have finished marinating, preheat the oven to 450°F.

4. Remove the breasts from the refrigerator. Turn the breasts meat side up and baste them with the marinade. Place the pan in the oven and bake for 10 minutes. Turn the breasts over, raise the oven temperature to 550°F, and bake for 10 minutes more, or until the breasts are done. The fat will have run off, and the skin will be brown and crisp at the edges.

5. Turn off the heat. Remove the pan from the oven and let the duck breasts rest for 10 minutes. Remove them to a platter and serve them with the sauce remaining in the pan. There should be 4 to 5 tablespoons.

NOTE The duck breasts can be covered and stored with their sauce in the refrigerator for up to 1 week, or frozen with their sauce for up to 6 weeks. Before using, thaw the breasts and allow to come to room temperature.

This simple stir-fry stars white asparagus, which is milder in flavor and more tender than the green kind. Instead of a brown sauce, which would hide the pretty spears, Lo opts for a light, gingery one.

STIR-FRIED BEEF TENDERLOIN WITH WHITE ASPARAGUS

MAKES 2 SERVINGS

- 1½ tablespoons oyster sauce
- 1 tablespoon Shaoxing wine
- 2 teaspoons toasted sesame oil
- 1½ teaspoons dark soy sauce
- 1 teaspoon rice vinegar
- 1 teaspoon sugar
- Pinch of white pepper
- 2½ teaspoons cornstarch
- Salt
- ½ pound beef tenderloin, very thinly sliced crosswise
- 3½ tablespoons peanut oil
- One ½-inch piece of ginger, peeled and lightly smashed
- 12 ounces white asparagus—trimmed, peeled and cut on the diagonal into ⅓-inch-thick slices
- 1 red bell pepper, cut into thin strips
- 1 large garlic clove, minced

EDITOR'S WINE CHOICE

Soft, blackberry-inflected Merlot: 2007 Nelms Road

1. In a medium bowl, mix the oyster sauce with the wine, sesame oil, soy sauce, rice vinegar, sugar, white pepper, 1½ teaspoons of the cornstarch and ¼ teaspoon of salt. Add the meat, toss to coat and let stand for 30 minutes.

2. In a small bowl, mix the remaining 1 teaspoon of cornstarch with 2 tablespoons of water.

3. Heat a wok until very hot. Add 1½ tablespoons of the peanut oil and heat until just smoking. Add the ginger and ¼ teaspoon of salt and fry the ginger for 15 seconds per side. Add the asparagus and bell pepper and stir-fry for 1 minute. Add 1 tablespoon of cold water and simmer for 30 seconds, until most of the water has evaporated. Scrape the vegetables into a bowl. Wipe out the wok.

4. Heat the remaining 2 tablespoons of peanut oil in the wok until smoking. Add the garlic and cook until fragrant, about 15 seconds. Add the meat and the marinade, spreading the meat in an even layer. Cook until the beef starts to brown slightly, about 1 minute. Turn and cook 1 minute longer. Return the vegetables to the wok and stir-fry until they are heated through and the meat is no longer pink, about 2 minutes. Add the cornstarch mixture and stir-fry for 1 minute, until the sauce thickens. Discard the ginger. Transfer the stir-fry to a bowl and serve.

SERVE WITH Steamed rice.

ITALIAN

CHICKEN WITH OLIVES
AND PINE NUTS, P. 231

LIDIA COOKS FROM THE HEART OF ITALY

Lidia Matticchio Bastianich &
Tanya Bastianich Manuali with David Nussbaum

So many people watch Lidia Bastianich's PBS cooking shows that she's really just Lidia now. In her sixth book, the companion to her TV series *Lidia's Italy*, Lidia celebrates lesser-known parts of the country like Basilicata. Basilicata's pantry is limited—pasta, cheese, vegetables, a little meat and fish—but cooks there might toss roasted tomatoes with spaghetti and bread crumbs to create a brilliant dish. Lidia, always a defender of the fresh and the slow, now permits a few shortcuts: To speed up her chicken with olives, she says, use breasts instead of a whole chicken. "Now I am relaxing a bit," she writes. "I want you to do the same."

Published by Alfred A. Knopf, $35

LIDIA COOKS FROM THE HEART OF ITALY
Lidia Matticchio Bastianich & Tanya Bastianich Manuali
with David Nussbaum

The basic, bright flavors in this Calabrian dish—crushed garlic, fresh lemon juice, chopped parsley—are appealing on delicate squid. Seek out small calamari, as they will be the most tender.

SPICY CALAMARI

SERVES 6

- 2 pounds cleaned calamari, whole bodies (skin on or off) and tentacles
- ¾ cup extra-virgin olive oil
- 6 plump garlic cloves, peeled and crushed
- 1½ teaspoons kosher salt
- ½ teaspoon peperoncino flakes, or to taste
- 2 tablespoons freshly squeezed lemon juice
- 1 tablespoon chopped fresh Italian parsley

RECOMMENDED EQUIPMENT
A heavy-bottomed skillet or sauté pan, 12-inch diameter or wider

EDITOR'S WINE CHOICE

**Citrusy, lightly sparkling
Prosecco: 2008 Bisson**

AUTHOR'S NOTE

I prefer to buy whole calamari and clean them myself (you can see how easy it is to do in my book *Lidia's Italian-American Kitchen*). I also like to leave the skin on the bodies—it takes on a lovely color when cooked. However, now that squid are frequently sold already cleaned, the body skin is usually peeled. If you like, ask the fishmonger to leave it on. The dish is marvelous either way.

It always pleases me when such a simple recipe can be so good. But every ingredient and every step must be perfect— the calamari, fresh; the olive oil, the best; and the pan must be hot for the quick cooking.

If you are not a fan of squid, you could also prepare scallops, swordfish, or even a fillet of cod using this recipe.

Dry the calamari well, and put in a large bowl. Pour over them ½ cup of the olive oil, and add the garlic, 1 teaspoon salt, and the peperoncino. Toss to coat and let marinate at room temperature for 30 minutes to an hour.

When you are ready to cook the calamari, make the dressing. In a small bowl, whisk together the remaining ¼ cup olive oil, the lemon juice, remaining ½ teaspoon salt, and the chopped parsley until emulsified.

Set the skillet over high heat, and when it is very hot, lift the calamari out of the marinade with tongs, let drain briefly, and then lay a batch of them flat in the dry skillet. Sear the calamari, turning several times, until the edges of the bodies and the tentacles are caramelized and crispy, about 2 minutes per batch. If you are using unskinned calamari, the skin will darken to a deep-reddish hue.

As the calamari come out of the skillet, arrange them on a warmed platter. When all of the calamari are done, drizzle the dressing over them, and serve right away.

LIDIA COOKS FROM THE HEART OF ITALY
Lidia Matticchio Bastianich & Tanya Bastianich Manuali
with David Nussbaum

This may be the perfect picnic salad: It's mayo-free and is delicious at room temperature. The use of giardiniera—mixed pickled vegetables sold ready-to-eat at the supermarket—is a great time-saver.

CHICKEN WITH GIARDINIERA

SERVES 6

FOR THE POACHED CHICKEN
One 3½-to-4-pound roasting chicken
1 medium onion, quartered through the root
1 large carrot, halved crosswise
1 large stalk celery, halved crosswise
2 fresh plum tomatoes
6 or so stalks fresh Italian parsley, with lots of leaves
1 tablespoon whole black peppercorns

FOR THE SALAD
3 cups giardiniera, store-bought or homemade, drained
One 6-ounce jar marinated artichoke hearts, drained
½ cup pitted oil-cured black olives
¼ cup chopped fresh Italian parsley
3 tablespoons small capers, drained
6 tablespoons extra-virgin olive oil, or more to taste
¼ cup red-wine vinegar, or more to taste
1½ teaspoons kosher salt, or more to taste

RECOMMENDED EQUIPMENT
A heavy-bottomed soup pot or saucepan, 8-quart or larger, with a cover

EDITOR'S WINE CHOICE
Zesty, full-bodied white:
2008 Palazzone Terre
Vineate Orvieto Classico

Giardiniera is a ubiquitous and versatile pantry staple in Umbria, as in other parts of Italy. It usually combines crisp chunks and slices of carrot, cauliflower, celery, and sweet or hot peppers; olives, onion, cucumbers, and turnips are in some brands of giardiniera, too. Embellished with freshly poached chicken, as in this recipe, giardiniera becomes a delicious and colorful dish, suitable as an appetizer at dinner, a main course for lunch, or a practical and appealing salad.

To poach the chicken

Rinse the bird; put it in the pot with the seasoning ingredients nestled around it. Pour over it cold water to cover, and bring to a boil, then cover the pot and adjust the heat to maintain a gentle simmer. Cook until the chicken is tender, 45 to 50 minutes.

Lift the chicken from the pot and set it in a colander or strainer over a bowl; let it cool. Remove the fat and skin, and discard. Take the meat off the bones, remove any cartilage or tendons, and tear the chicken into nice salad-sized shreds (about ½ inch wide and 2 inches long)—you should have about 5 cups chicken pieces. (If you want to finish the stock to put away, return the bones, cartilage, and the broth to the pot; simmer for another hour or more. Strain and cool it, then refrigerate or freeze.)

To assemble the salad

Toss the chicken, giardiniera, artichokes, olives, parsley, and capers in a large bowl. Drizzle over it the olive oil and vinegar; toss to coat all the salad pieces. Taste, and adjust the seasoning with salt, olive oil, or vinegar. Give it a final toss, and serve.

In this recipe from Le Marche, Bastianich uses an unconventional stovetop method for browning the chicken, using low heat and a covered pan. This keeps the meat moist while crisping the skin.

CHICKEN WITH OLIVES & PINE NUTS

SERVES 6

3½ to 4 pounds assorted cut-up
    chicken pieces
1 teaspoon kosher salt
2 tablespoons extra-virgin olive oil
2 tablespoons butter
3 plump garlic cloves, peeled
2 bay leaves, preferably fresh
1 cup brine-cured green Italian
    olives or oil-cured black
    Italian olives
½ cup white wine
¼ cup toasted pine nuts

RECOMMENDED EQUIPMENT
A 12-inch cast-iron or other
    heavy skillet or sauté pan,
    with a cover
An olive pitter

EDITOR'S WINE CHOICE

**Herbal, minerally white:
2008 Sartarelli Classico
Verdicchio**

AUTHOR'S NOTE

If you're using small olives like Castelvetrano, use a pitter and keep them whole. If you have larger olives (such as Ascolane or Cerignola), smash them with the blade of a chef's knife to remove the pits, and break them into coarse chunks.

Rinse the chicken pieces and pat dry. Trim off excess skin and all visible fat. Cut drumsticks off the thighs; cut breast halves into two pieces each. Season the chicken all over with the salt.

Put the olive oil and butter in the pan, and set over medium-low heat. When the butter is melted and hot, lay in the chicken pieces, skin side down, in a single layer; drop the garlic cloves and bay leaves in the spaces between them.

Cover the pan; let the chicken cook over gentle heat, browning slowly and releasing its fat and juices. After about 10 minutes, uncover the pan, turn the pieces, and move them around the pan to cook evenly, then replace the cover. Turn again in 10 minutes or so, and continue cooking covered.

While the chicken is browning, pit the olives (if they still have pits in them; see Author's Note).

After the chicken has cooked for 30 minutes, scatter the olives onto the pan bottom, around the chicken, and pour in the wine. Raise the heat so the liquid is bubbling, cover, and cook, gradually concentrating the juices, for about 5 minutes.

Cook uncovered, evaporating the pan juices, occasionally turning the chicken and olives. If there is a lot of fat in the pan, tilt the skillet and spoon off the fat from one side.

Scatter the pine nuts around the chicken, and continue cooking uncovered, turning the chicken over gently until the pan juices thicken and coat the meat like a glaze.

Serve the chicken from the skillet, or on a platter. Spoon out any sauce left in the pan, and drizzle over the chicken.

Cooks in the mountainous region of Basilicata are ingenious at using inexpensive ingredients. The bread crumbs in this recipe, for instance, both add crunch and thicken the sauce.

PASTA WITH BAKED CHERRY TOMATOES

SERVES 6

- 3 pints cherry tomatoes, halved
- ½ cup plus 1 tablespoon extra-virgin olive oil
- ⅓ cup fine dry bread crumbs
- 1 teaspoon kosher salt, plus more for the pasta pot
- ¼ teaspoon peperoncino flakes, or to taste
- 1 pound spaghetti, gemelli, or penne
- 10 plump garlic cloves, peeled and sliced
- 2 tablespoons chopped fresh Italian parsley
- 1 cup loosely packed fresh basil leaves, shredded
- ½ cup freshly grated pecorino (or half pecorino and half Grana Padano or Parmigiano-Reggiano), plus more for passing
- 4 ounces ricotta or ricotta salata

RECOMMENDED EQUIPMENT

A large, rimmed sheet pan lined with parchment paper

A large pot, 8-quart capacity, for cooking the pasta

A heavy-bottomed skillet or sauté pan, 12-inch diameter or larger

The deep flavor and delightfully varied textures of this pasta dressing develop in the oven, where you bake the cherry tomatoes coated with bread crumbs just before you toss them with pasta. Roasting them this way intensifies their flavor, and the bread crumbs become crunchy. It is a lovely dish to make when sweet cherry tomatoes are in season, but it is also good with the lesser cherry-tomato varieties you get in winter; these can be used successfully here because of the concentration of taste and texture during baking.

This dressing is suitable for almost any pasta, but I particularly like it with spaghetti, gemelli, or penne. Because the tomatoes are at their best as soon as they come out of the oven, the dressing and pasta should be cooked simultaneously, and I have written the recipe to ensure that you will have your pasta and baked tomatoes ready for each other at the same time.

Arrange a rack in the center of the oven, and heat to 350°F.

Toss the cherry-tomato halves in a large bowl with 3 tablespoons of the olive oil. Sprinkle over tomatoes the bread crumbs, salt, and peperoncino; toss well to coat the tomatoes evenly. Pour the tomatoes onto the parchment-lined sheet, and spread them apart in a single layer. Bake until the tomatoes are shriveled and lightly caramelized (but not dried out), about 25 minutes in all.

continued on p. 234

ITALIAN

LIDIA COOKS FROM THE HEART OF ITALY

Lidia Matticchio Bastianich & Tanya Bastianich Manuali
with David Nussbaum

EDITOR'S WINE CHOICE

**Juicy, lemony white: 2008 Sella
& Mosca La Cala Vermentino**

Meanwhile, fill the large pot with salted water, and heat to a rolling boil. When the tomatoes are nearly done, drop the pasta into the pot, stir, and return the water to a boil.

As soon as the pasta is cooking, pour the remaining olive oil into the big skillet, set it over medium-high heat, and scatter in the sliced garlic. Cook for a minute or two, until it is sizzling and lightly colored, then ladle in about 2 cups of the pasta cooking water, and bring to a vigorous boil, stirring up the garlic. Let half the water evaporate, then lower the heat, stir in the chopped parsley, and keep the sauce barely simmering.

As soon as the tomatoes are done, remove them from the oven.

When the pasta is *al dente,* lift it from the water, drain for a moment, and drop it into the skillet, still over low heat. Toss pasta quickly with the garlic-and-parsley sauce in the pan, then slide the baked tomatoes on top of the pasta. Scatter the basil shreds all over, and toss everything together well, until the pasta is evenly dressed and the tomatoes are distributed throughout. Turn off the heat, sprinkle on the grated cheese, and toss once more.

Mound the pasta in a warmed serving bowl. Shred the ricotta all over the top of the pasta, and serve immediately.

An adaptation of a recipe from *Lidia's Family Table,* this masterful combination of salty and sweet is a signature dish at the New York City restaurant Felidia. The homemade pasta is well worth the effort.

FRESH PEAR & PECORINO RAVIOLI

SERVES 6

2⅔ cups all-purpose flour, plus more for dusting
½ teaspoon salt
4 large eggs, lightly beaten
1 teaspoon extra-virgin olive oil
3 firm Bartlett pears (1 pound)— peeled, halved, cored and coarsely grated
8 ounces fresh pecorino cheese, coarsely grated (3 cups)
4 ounces aged pecorino cheese, finely grated (1⅓ cups), plus more for serving
3 tablespoons mascarpone cheese
1½ sticks (6 ounces) unsalted butter
Freshly ground pepper

EDITOR'S WINE CHOICE
Floral, fruity white:
2008 Conte Brandolini
Tocai Friulano

LIDIA BASTIANICH ONLINE
lidiasitaly.com
f Lidia Bastianich

1. In a food processor, pulse the 2⅔ cups flour with the salt. With the machine on, add the eggs and oil; process until the dough forms a ball. Transfer the dough to a work surface; knead until smooth and elastic, about 5 minutes. Flatten the dough into a disk, wrap in plastic and let stand at room temperature for at least 30 minutes or refrigerate for up to 1 day.

2. Meanwhile, in a bowl, mix the pears with the fresh pecorino, 4 ounces aged pecorino and the mascarpone. Refrigerate.

3. Cut the dough into 6 equal pieces; work with one piece at a time and keep the rest wrapped. Flatten the dough with your hands and run it through successively narrower settings on a pasta machine until you reach the thinnest. You should have a sheet of dough that is 5½ inches by 24 inches. Lightly dust the bottom of the pasta sheet with flour. Spoon 8 tablespoon-size dollops of the filling along the bottom half of the long side of the dough, spacing them out evenly. Dip your fingers in water and moisten the bottom edge of the dough and between the mounds of filling. Fold the top half of the dough over the filling and press out any air pockets. Using a sharp knife, cut the dough between the filling into ravioli. Transfer the ravioli to a lightly floured baking sheet and cover with plastic wrap. Repeat with the remaining pasta dough and filling.

4. Bring a large pot of salted water to a boil. Add the ravioli and boil just until the pasta is al dente, about 3 minutes. Drain.

5. Meanwhile, in a large skillet, melt the butter with ½ cup of water. Add the ravioli and toss gently to coat with the butter. Season generously with pepper. Transfer the ravioli to shallow bowls and serve, passing grated aged pecorino at the table.

PASTA E FAGIOLI, P. 238

SALT TO TASTE

Marco Canora with Catherine Young

arco Canora's farmers' market–inspired, rustic-refined Italian food at Hearth and Terroir in New York City has earned him a passionate, well-deserved following. Fans will adore his first cookbook, too, because Canora explains all the small decisions he makes as he cooks. For instance, when he renders prosciutto and bacon for his version of the bean soup Pasta e Fagioli, he leaves the fat in the pot; the beans, he says, need the flavor. His tips anticipate a cook's questions, explaining why it's best to hold off on seasoning a sauce, say, or how to keep meatballs from crumbling (freeze them before cooking). Canora offers exquisite recipes, but more important, he makes sure readers truly understand how to prepare them.

Published by Rodale, $35

For his Pasta e Fagioli, Canora purees half the beans before adding them to the pot. It's an unusually lush take on the classic soup.

PASTA E FAGIOLI

SERVES 6

- 4 ounces prosciutto or pancetta, cut into 4 pieces (see Author's Note on p. 239)
- 4 ounces smoked slab bacon, cut into 4 pieces
- 6 tablespoons extra-virgin olive oil plus additional for serving
- 2 cups diced white onions
- Kosher salt and freshly ground black pepper
- 2 tablespoons minced garlic
- 1½ tablespoons finely chopped fresh rosemary
- 1½ tablespoons finely chopped fresh sage
- 1½ tablespoons tomato paste
- 2¾ cups Brodo (p. 245) or chicken broth
- 3 cups cooked borlotti or other beans, cooking liquid reserved (or one 28-ounce can, rinsed)
- 1 pound dried short tubular pasta, such as ditalini or elbow macaroni
- 3 tablespoons unsalted butter
- 2 tablespoons freshly grated Parmigiano-Reggiano

AUTHOR'S NOTE

There will be quite a bit of fat in the pot after you render the meat, but don't discard it; you need every bit of it to flavor the beans and broth.

I've had many versions of this dish over the years, and the thing that varies most is the consistency. I've had "fagioli" served as a thin broth with pasta, a hearty pasta dressed with a sauce of beans and puree, and almost everything in between. There's no right way. Use the puree, thinning or thickening it, to get things the way you want them. Personally, I like pasta e fagioli that's hearty—more a pasta dish than a soup. If you do too, follow the recipe as is; if not, add more broth. Either way, do add a little broth just before serving (the pasta and beans keep on absorbing liquid as they sit, so I always add a little fresh broth to get the consistency right and to wake up the flavor).

Combine the prosciutto or pancetta, bacon, and oil in a large pot. Cook over medium heat, turning the pieces regularly, until the fat renders. When the meat begins to brown, about 7 minutes, add the onions. Season with salt and pepper and stir to coat the onions with the sizzling fat. Fry the onions, stirring occasionally, until they are soft and begin to color, about 10 minutes more.

Add the garlic and cook, stirring occasionally, until it is soft and fragrant, about 3 minutes. Then add the rosemary and sage.

Cook for a minute or two, then stir in the tomato paste. Reduce the heat to medium-low and cook the mixture until it concentrates and darkens, about 5 minutes. Add the broth and half of the beans to the pot and bring to a simmer over medium heat.

EDITOR'S WINE CHOICE

Vibrant, cherry-scented Dolcetto d'Alba: 2008 Giovanni Rosso Le Quattro Vigne

AUTHOR'S NOTE

You want to cut the pork into pieces to maximize the surface area of the meat that will be exposed to heat. This increases the amount of flavor you can extract to flavor the beans. But don't cut the pieces too small or they will be hard to retrieve when the time comes.

Meanwhile, puree the remaining beans in a blender or food processor with just enough of the bean cooking liquid or water to allow the blade to rotate, about ¾ cup (you want the bean puree to be as thick as possible). Scrape the puree into the pot and stir to mix thoroughly. Simmer until the flavors blend, about 10 minutes.

Remove the pieces of cured meat and discard them. Season the bean mixture with salt and pepper and keep warm over low heat. Or you can cool and refrigerate or freeze the beans for later use.

About 10 minutes before you plan to serve, cook the pasta in a large pot of boiling salted water. When it's almost al dente, lift the pasta from the boiling water and add it to the bean mixture. Stir in the butter and Parmigiano. Add a few grinds of pepper and simmer until the pasta is done. Ladle the pasta e fagioli into warm bowls and serve drizzled with oil.

These cute little dumplings—in texture, a cross between a meatball and a matzo ball—are a simple combination of ground chicken, egg, cream and seasonings. They make the soup a terrific meal in a bowl.

CHICKEN SOUP WITH FARRO & DUMPLINGS

SERVES 6 TO 8

FOR THE DUMPLINGS
- 1 pound ground chicken
- 1 egg
- 2 teaspoons very finely chopped fresh rosemary
- ⅓ cup freshly grated Parmigiano-Reggiano
- ¼ teaspoon freshly grated nutmeg
- Kosher salt and freshly ground black pepper
- ¼ cup heavy cream

FOR THE SOUP
- 2 tablespoons extra-virgin olive oil plus additional for serving
- 2 cups diced onions
- 1 cup diced carrots
- 1 cup diced celery
- Kosher salt and freshly ground black pepper
- 1 medium head of escarole, wilted leaves and core discarded, leaves chopped
- 12 cups Brodo (p. 245) or other rich homemade broth
- 2 cups cooked Farro (recipe follows)
- Freshly grated Parmigiano-Reggiano

AUTHOR'S NOTE
I think piping the dumplings out is the way to go, but you could also drop teaspoonfuls of the chicken mixture into the broth.

Odd as it may seem, the inspiration for this soup was not a cherished family recipe but canned Progresso Chickarina Soup. I loved it as a child, and when I opened Hearth, I wanted to make my own version. The dumplings, really tender chicken meatballs, are poached in broth, and I added escarole and farro to my notion of the original recipe. It's a very soothing soup and not hard to make, but be aware that the quality of the broth is key.

To make the dumplings

Place the chicken, egg, rosemary, Parmigiano, and nutmeg in a food processor. Season with salt and lots of pepper and pulse until mixed, adding the cream gradually. Spoon the mixture into a piping bag or a resealable plastic bag (if you snip a corner, this will work just as well). Chill the dumpling mixture.

To make the soup

Heat the oil in a large pot over medium heat. Add the onions, carrots, and celery. Season with salt and pepper and mix well. Cover and sweat the vegetables (cook them until they are soft but have not yet begun to color), stirring occasionally, about 10 minutes.

Add the escarole, stir to coat with oil, reduce the heat to low, and cook, stirring occasionally, until the escarole starts to wilt, about 5 minutes.

continued on p. 242

ITALIAN

SALT TO TASTE
Marco Canora with Catherine Young

EDITOR'S WINE NOTE

Fleshy, green apple–inflected Spanish white: 2008 Bodegas Godeval Godello

AUTHOR'S NOTE

In the fall and winter, I like a heartier flavor, so I render some chopped pancetta or prosciutto and use the fat to brown rather than sweat the aromatic vegetables. You can also cook the farro in stock rather than water for a richer taste.

Add the broth and farro. Bring the soup to a boil over high heat. Once again lower the heat. Simmer until the escarole is very soft, about 20 minutes. Season with salt and pepper.

Squeeze small dumplings (about the size of your thumb tip) from the bag into the simmering broth. Cover the pot and let the dumplings poach until they are firm, 10 minutes. Serve topped with Parmigiano, lots of black pepper, and oil.

The soup will keep in the refrigerator for days and freezes beautifully.

FARRO

You can use farro pretty much any way you would rice. Serve it plain as a sustaining side dish, treat it like Arborio rice to make risotto-like farrotto, or add it to soup. From a cook's standpoint, farro is great because it stops absorbing liquid when it's tender—this means it doesn't turn to mush in the pot.

To make about 5 cups of cooked farro, heat 2 tablespoons of extra-virgin olive oil in a large pot over medium-low heat. Chop, then add 1 small onion, 1 small carrot, and 1 small stalk of celery. Season with salt and pepper and stir the vegetables to coat them with the oil. Cover the pot and lower the heat. Cook the vegetables until they soften, about 10 minutes.

Add 2 cups of farro. Stir to coat it with the oil and vegetable juices. Add enough water to cover by about ½ inch. Raise the heat and bring the water to a boil, then adjust the heat so the farro simmers.

Cook the farro until it is tender, about 20 minutes, adding more water if the pot looks dry. Remove and discard the aromatic vegetables. Serve warm as you would rice or at room temperature.

Canora extracts maximum flavor from corn by steeping the cobs in broth, then uses the infused broth for the risotto. Adding butter and Parmigiano-Reggiano just before serving makes the rice ultracreamy.

CORN & PANCETTA RISOTTO

SERVES 6 TO 8

¼ pound thinly sliced pancetta
4 ears of corn, husked
6 to 8 cups Brodo (recipe follows) or chicken broth
Kosher salt and freshly ground black pepper
4 tablespoons (½ stick) unsalted butter
About 2 tablespoons extra-virgin olive oil
1 large onion, peeled and diced
2 cups Arborio or other short-grained rice
¾ cup dry white wine
½ cup freshly grated Parmigiano-Reggiano

AUTHOR'S NOTE
If you like, you can render the pancetta in your pot, then add the onion and rice to start the risotto. Made this way, the dish will have a more assertively meaty flavor—perfect with grilled corn.

Corn and pancetta risotto can be made a number of ways, all equally good. The corn can be precooked—grilled or sweated in butter—then added with the last ladle of broth. Or if it's fresh, young, and tender, you can add raw corn a bit earlier in the process.

Preheat the oven to 400°F. Divide the pancetta between 2 rimmed baking sheets, laying it out in a single layer. Bake the pancetta until the fat renders and the meat is beginning to crisp, 7 to 10 minutes. Pour off the rendered fat and reserve it. Chop the pancetta; add the chopped pancetta to the fat and set the mixture aside.

While the pancetta cooks, cut the corn from the cobs. Reserve the corn kernels; break the cobs in half and put them in a large pot. Add the broth and bring to a simmer over high heat. Reduce the heat slightly and simmer until the broth has reduced by one-third, about 30 minutes. Remove and discard the cobs. Season the broth lightly with salt and pepper and reserve.

Melt 2 tablespoons butter in a rondeau or high-sided skillet over medium heat. Add enough oil so the bottom of the pan is generously coated, about 2 tablespoons. Add the onion, season with salt and pepper, and cook, stirring occasionally, until it softens, about 10 minutes.

continued on p. 244

SALT TO TASTE
Marco Canora with Catherine Young

AUTHOR'S NOTE
Try adding chopped fresh herbs when you add the butter. I think basil goes particularly well with corn.

Increase the heat to high and add the rice. Using a wooden spoon, stir the rice with the onion and fat until the rice no longer looks chalky and the grains begin to crackle, 2 to 3 minutes.

Make sure the pan is really hot, then add the wine. The wine will almost immediately begin to boil. Stir constantly until the rice absorbs the wine, about 1 minute.

Add enough warm broth to just cover the rice, 1½ to 2 cups. Cook at an active simmer, stirring and scraping the rice away from the sides occasionally. As the rice cooks, the broth will become viscous. Cook the rice until it is once again almost dry, about 5 minutes. Then again add enough broth to cover. Add the raw corn and simmer, scraping and stirring every so often, until the broth is incorporated, about 5 minutes more. (The risotto can be made several hours ahead up to this point. Simply spread the hot rice on a baking sheet and cool. Cover and refrigerate until ready to reheat and complete the recipe.)

At this point, add the pancetta and fat and no more than ½ cup broth. Stir frequently and add broth in small increments until the rice is just tender. Depending upon the age of the rice and how soft and brothy you like your risotto, you can expect to add 1 to 2 cups more in all. Just take care to go slowly so you don't add too much.

Stir in the Parmigiano and the remaining 2 tablespoons butter. Taste and adjust the seasoning with salt and pepper and serve.

AUTHOR'S NOTE

Brodo is not stock, but broth. Stock is made from simmering bones, and broth is made from simmering meat. The practical difference is that stock contains more gelatin and is therefore an easier starting place for sauces. Because broths are made with whole pieces of meat and poultry rather than bones, they usually have deeper, more complex flavor. Broths also tend to be less cloudy—the protein in the meats in the pot acts as a filter that clarifies the broth as it simmers, leaving you with a beautifully clear liquid.

BRODO

Brodo is easy to make with ingredients from the supermarket. Start with a chicken. Put it whole in the pot, then add 2 pounds of beef stew meat on the bone and a turkey drumstick (or two wings). Cover the meat by about 4 inches with water (you'll need about 7 quarts in all) and bring it to a boil over high heat.

As soon as the broth boils, begin to "clarify" it, lowering the heat to medium and pulling the pot to one side of the burner so it's partially off the burner. This forces the broth to boil in an oval circuit from top to bottom, circulating all the liquid over and around the meat. As the broth circulates, the fat and other impurities in the broth float to the surface. What will you see when you look into the pot? The broth will bubble along one side of the pot. The rest of the surface will look active but not be bubbling. Fat and scum will rise with the bubbles and settle on the top.

Skim every 5 minutes or so. Be finicky about how you do this. Dip the ladle into the broth near the center of the pot just deep enough to barely submerge the front edge. Then keep it still. A thin stream of fat and foamy broth will be drawn into the ladle. Do this a couple of times, then wait another 5 minutes and do it again, continuing until the brodo looks clear, about half an hour.

Once the broth is clear, add aromatic vegetables. Chop and then add 2 onions, ½ bunch of celery, and 3 carrots. Add a 12-ounce can of tomatoes, 1 teaspoon peppercorns, and ½ bunch of flat-leaf parsley and simmer the broth until it's flavorful, about 2 hours.

Strain the broth; discard the vegetables but not the meat. (In my mind, brodo is forever linked with polpettone, the fried morsels of minced meat that, in my family, give a second life to the chicken, beef, and turkey used in the broth.) You'll wind up with 3½ quarts of broth that can be refrigerated or frozen.

An example of the smart tips in this book: To help the bass in these parchment packets (*al cartoccio*) cook speedily, Canora preheats the baking sheet so the fish starts to roast the second it's in the oven.

STRIPED BASS AL CARTOCCIO

SERVES 4

- 3 tablespoons extra-virgin olive oil
- Kosher salt and freshly ground black pepper
- 8 fresh rosemary sprigs
- 1 lemon, thinly sliced
- 1 skinless striped bass fillet (2 pounds), about ½ inch thick, cut into four 8-ounce pieces
- ¼ cup Niçoise olives, pitted if desired
- 2 large shallots, peeled and sliced as thinly as possible
- 2 tablespoons finely chopped fresh flat-leaf parsley

EDITOR'S WINE CHOICE

Minerally, fruity rosé:
2009 Domaine Sainte Lucie
Made In Provence Classic

AUTHOR'S NOTE

When I cook striped bass or other fish with thick skin, I remove it. Thin-skinned fish like black bass can be cooked with the skin on.

This is a flavorful, healthy way to cook fish. The basic formula is to create a packet for the fish out of parchment (aluminum foil also works), then add flavorings. The fish winds up perfectly steamed. When you pull the package open, it's so aromatic that I like to bring the fish in the parchment to the table and serve it there. You can wrap and steam each serving individually, or steam all the fish in one packet, but either way, I suggest you cut the fillets into portions first to make serving it easier.

Preheat the oven to 400°F. Place a baking sheet in the oven to heat.

Meanwhile, cut 4 large pieces (16 by 12½ inches) of parchment and place them on a clean work surface. Fold the parchment piece in half, then cut each in a half oval. Unfold the parchment, brush each piece with a little oil, then sprinkle with salt and pepper. Lay 2 sprigs of rosemary and a few lemon slices on each piece. Top with a portion of fish. Season the fish with salt and pepper and then put the remaining lemon slices on top. Scatter the olives over the fish. Separate the sliced shallots into rings and put them on the fish as well. Drizzle the remaining oil over all, then sprinkle with the parsley.

continued on p. 248

AUTHOR'S NOTE

Virtually any fish can be cooked this way, with only slight alterations in the method. The trick is that because the fish is enclosed in parchment, it can be hard to tell when it is done, the time ranging from less than 5 minutes to as much as 30. Really delicate fillets like sole and flounder will cook the most quickly, the exact time depending on the size of the fillet. With larger, denser fish, I cut thick fillets on the bias into medallions as this reduces the cooking time. It also increases the surface area, so flavorings have more impact on the finished dish.

Seal the fish in the pouches—you want to fold one half over the other, then gather the two sides together and fold and crimp the edges tightly enough to seal—think Jiffy Pop. Put the packet on the preheated baking sheet and steam the fish in the oven until it is tender, about 15 minutes. (You can check by giving the fish in the foil a squeeze; if it gives easily, then it's done. If you're not sure, it's okay to peek; just open the packet up as little as possible and close it up quickly if the fish isn't ready.)

Variations

A few flavoring additions worth considering: white or red wine or vermouth; garlic; tarragon; thyme; basil; spices like coriander, mustard, or bay. Or try adding artichokes, potatoes, mushrooms, truffles, tomatoes, leeks, fennel, or celery. Just remember to cut vegetables small enough to cook quickly, and precook veggies (like artichokes and potatoes) that need more time than the fish will take to cook.

BEST OF THE BEST EXCLUSIVE

This creamless soup gets its silky texture from slowly roasted fennel, which essentially melts once it's pureed.

ROASTED FENNEL SOUP WITH HAZELNUTS

SERVES 8

- 8 large fennel bulbs (about 8 pounds), trimmed and cut into 8 wedges each
- 3 large onions, cut into 8 wedges each
- Four 4-inch rosemary sprigs
- ½ cup extra-virgin olive oil
- Kosher salt and freshly ground pepper
- ⅓ cup blanched hazelnuts
- 10 cups chicken stock or low-sodium broth

1. Preheat the oven to 375°F. In a large roasting pan, toss the fennel with the onions, rosemary sprigs and olive oil and season with salt and pepper. Roast for about 45 minutes, tossing halfway through, until the fennel is tender and browned in spots. Discard the rosemary sprigs.

2. Meanwhile, spread the hazelnuts in a pie plate and toast for about 8 minutes, until golden and fragrant. Let cool, then coarsely chop the hazelnuts.

3. Scrape the vegetables and any juices into a large soup pot. Add the chicken stock and bring to a simmer. Cover and simmer over low heat until the vegetables are very tender, about 35 minutes.

4. In a blender, carefully puree the soup in batches until smooth. Strain the soup through a fine-mesh sieve into a clean pot. Reheat the soup and season with salt and pepper. Ladle into warmed bowls, sprinkle with the hazelnuts and serve.

MAKE AHEAD The soup can be refrigerated for up to 3 days. Reheat before serving.

MARCO CANORA ONLINE
restauranthearth.com
Hearth Restaurant
@marcomostarda

SEARED TUNA WITH SWEET-
SOUR ONIONS, P. 254

SEAFOOD ALLA SICILIANA

Toni Lydecker

Sicilians know how to cook fish the way God meant it to be cooked." Toni Lydecker quotes Inspector Montalbano, the protagonist of a popular series of Italian detective stories, to explain why she wrote this book. A specialist in Italian regional cuisines, Lydecker investigates Sicily's complicated history, with its centuries of Greek, Arab, French and Spanish invasions, and details the island's short list of phenomenal core ingredients (including olive oil, sea salt, capers, anchovies and tomatoes). She presents alluring, easy-to-follow recipes—like rare-seared tuna in a perfectly balanced sauce of vinegar and sweet red onions—and offers insights into the local culture. All make this a uniquely satisfying cookbook.

Published by Lake Isle Press, $38

The vibrant topping here would complement any number of steamed vegetables, such as green beans or broccoli.

ASPARAGUS WITH TOMATO-OLIVE GARNISH

MAKES 4 TO 6 SERVINGS
PREP 15 MINUTES
COOK 5 MINUTES

  1 small tomato, peeled, seeded, and diced, or ½ cup quartered cherry tomatoes
  4 Mediterranean olives, pitted and chopped
2 to 3 tablespoons crumbled ricotta salata or feta cheese
Extra-virgin olive oil
  1 pound asparagus, ends trimmed (see Author's Note)
Sea salt or kosher salt
Freshly ground black pepper (optional)

AUTHOR'S NOTE

Peeling the bottom half of asparagus stems is optional but adds a note of elegance that seems fitting for this dish. It's especially nice with thick asparagus spears.

Asparagus, seasoned simply with olive oil, salt, and perhaps a squeeze of lemon juice, is a natural companion for almost any seafood dish. This variation is for occasions—or moods—that call for an extra flourish.

Combine the tomato, olives, and cheese in a small bowl. Toss with a little olive oil.

Simmer the asparagus in salted boiling water until barely tender (alternatively, steam the asparagus); drain. Arrange the spears on a serving platter, drizzle with olive oil, and sprinkle lightly with salt and, if desired, pepper. Spoon the tomato-olive garnish across the center of the asparagus. Serve at room temperature.

Variation

Asparagus with Mushroom-Cheese Garnish: Trim and chop 4 white or cremini mushrooms (about 1 cup). Sauté the mushrooms and 2 tablespoons finely chopped onion in 1 tablespoon olive oil until soft; season lightly with salt. Off heat, stir in 2 to 3 tablespoons crumbled ricotta salata or feta cheese. Prepare the asparagus as described in the recipe, substituting the mushroom-cheese garnish. Serve warm or at room temperature.

SEAFOOD ALLA SICILIANA
Toni Lydecker

Just a few simple ingredients come together here for a terrific dish. Lydecker cooks red onion in vinegar, sugar, salt and water, then piles it onto seared tuna steaks with plenty of fresh mint.

SEARED TUNA WITH SWEET-SOUR ONIONS

MAKES 3 OR 4 SERVINGS
PREP 10 MINUTES
COOK 20 MINUTES

   1 large tuna steak at least 1 inch thick (about 1 pound), cut into 3 or 4 portions
Sea salt or kosher salt
Freshly ground black pepper (optional)
   5 tablespoons red wine vinegar
   1 tablespoon sugar, or to taste
   1 large red onion, cut pole to pole into thin wedges
Extra-virgin olive oil
Several mint leaves, snipped into ribbons

EDITOR'S WINE CHOICE

Rich, tropical Sicilian white:
2008 Planeta Cometa

Here's a variation on the agrodolce *theme, based loosely on a recipe from Charly, chef of Taormina's Vicolo Stretto restaurant. With red onion crowning each tuna steak, it looks pretty and makes an especially nice warm-weather dish, served at room temperature—like most sweet-sour dishes, the taste improves once the tuna and onions have had a chance to spend time together.*

Season the tuna on both sides with salt and, if using, pepper. In a small bowl, mix the vinegar, sugar, and a pinch of salt with ¼ cup water.

In a heavy-bottomed skillet (such as cast iron), combine the onion with a little olive oil. Cook over medium-low heat, covered, until soft, about 10 minutes. Add the sweet-sour mixture, stirring often as the liquid evaporates and the onions begin to caramelize. Transfer to a bowl.

Clean the skillet, add 1 tablespoon olive oil, and raise the heat to medium. Sear the tuna until well browned. Turn the steaks and pile the onions on top. As soon as the second side is browned, reduce the heat and add a little water. Simmer a minute or so more for medium rare, a little longer for medium.

Transfer the tuna to dinner plates. Deglaze the pan by adding a little water and cook until thickened; drizzle over the onion-topped tuna steaks. Sprinkle with the mint. Serve warm or at room temperature.

For this clever "pizza-panino," Lydecker partially bakes pizza dough (homemade or store-bought), slices it horizontally, fills it with cheese, tomatoes and anchovies, then puts it back in the oven.

PIZZA-PANINO WITH ANCHOVIES & TOMATOES

MAKES 3 OR 4 SERVINGS
PREP 10 MINUTES
COOK 12 MINUTES

Extra-virgin olive oil
  1 pound pizza dough, homemade
       (recipe follows) or purchased
Unbleached all-purpose flour,
       for dusting
10 to 12 anchovies, pinched into
       several pieces
  1 large tomato, sliced
Dried oregano
6 to 8 thin deli slices young
       pecorino or provolone cheese
  2 cups microgreens
Fresh lemon juice or wine vinegar
Sea salt or kosher salt

AUTHOR'S NOTE

To improve the chances of achieving a crisp crust, buy half a dozen unglazed quarry tiles, available from a home supply store. Line a middle rack of the oven with the tiles before preheating the oven. Place the pizza pan on top of the tiles and, midway through the cooking, after the crust has firmed up, slide the pizza out of the pan and onto the tiles to finish cooking.

Never mind that schiacciata *is the local name for focaccia in Tuscany. Palermo defines the word differently, and it is this version that chef Salvatore Fraterrigo makes at New York's Cacio e Vino. The dough is baked halfway, split, filled, and baked once more to make a delicious something that walks the line between pizza and panino. Salvatore is originally from Trapani, where ordering a* cabuccio *will also get you the same thing. In the small town near Palermo where Giusto Priola, his partner, grew up, this pizza-panino went by the name* faccia da vecchia *(old woman's face), an allusion to its leathery look after baking. "We ate this mostly in the fall," he remembers. "When the new oil comes in, it's a little spicy at first, and you don't need a filling, just the oil and a little oregano. My grandmother made it that way." The variation I've included, made with steamed escarole, was inspired by* calzoni *typical of Messina. Naturally, these have another name:* piduni.

Preheat the oven to 500°F. (See Author's Note for baking hints.) Lightly brush a pizza pan or rimmed baking sheet with olive oil.

Divide the pizza dough in half, dusting the pieces lightly with flour to make them easier to handle. On a pastry board or other smooth surface, roll or pat 1 piece to make an 8-inch round about the size and shape of a pita. Transfer to the prepared pan, and brush lightly with olive oil. Repeat with the other piece of dough. Bake on a center rack for 5 minutes.

continued on p. 257

Slide the partially cooked pizzas onto the pastry board. Press the tops firmly with a spatula to deflate. Using a long serrated knife, carefully cut horizontally in half (see Note below).

On 2 halves, arrange the anchovies and top with the tomatoes. Sprinkle with oregano and drizzle lightly with olive oil. Cover with the cheese, tearing the slices as needed to fit. Place the other pizza halves on top. Brush lightly with olive oil.

Return the stuffed pizzas to the oven for 7 minutes, or until the cheese melts and the top is lightly browned (if it fails to brown, turn on the broiler briefly). Cut each stuffed pizza into 6 wedges and arrange on plates. Toss the microgreens with a little olive oil, lemon juice, and salt; mound in the center.

NOTE The safest method is to saw around the edges, 1 or 2 inches in, before cutting the center part. To repair any damage caused by cutting too deeply, trim off a thicker part of the cut side and patch the hole; use the intact half on the bottom.

Variation

Pizza-Panino with Escarole, Anchovies and Sun-Dried Tomatoes: Prepare, partially bake, and split the dough as described in the recipe. Meanwhile, steam 4 cups shredded escarole in a covered saucepan or microwave dish. Drain well; you should have about 1 cup. To stuff the pizzas: Distribute 6 to 8 anchovies, in pieces, over the bottom halves; sprinkle with 6 sun-dried tomatoes snipped into thin slices with kitchen shears. Cover with the steamed escarole. Drizzle lightly with olive oil. Top with the cheese and finish baking as described.

continued on p. 258

SEAFOOD ALLA SICILIANA
Toni Lydecker

PIZZA DOUGH

This versatile dough is suitable for thin-crust pizza or stuffed schiacciata.

**MAKES 1 POUND DOUGH
(TWO 12-INCH PIZZAS)
PREP 15 MINUTES
(PLUS 1½ HOURS RISING TIME)**

2½ teaspoons (1 envelope) active
    dry yeast
Extra-virgin olive oil
  2 cups unbleached all-purpose
    flour, plus more as needed
  1 teaspoon sea salt or other
    finely ground salt

Combine the yeast with 1 cup warm water (110°F to 115°F) in a liquid measuring cup. Let stand for a few minutes, until a beige scum forms on top. Add 2 tablespoons olive oil.

Whisk together 2 cups flour and the salt in a large mixing bowl. Add the yeast mixture, stirring with a plastic spatula until most of the flour is incorporated. Turn the dough onto a pastry board or other surface lightly dusted with flour. Knead the dough, adding up to ½ cup more flour as needed, until soft but elastic and only slightly sticky. Form into a ball.

Clean the bowl and drizzle a little oil into it; turn the dough in the oil to coat lightly. Cover and let rise in a warm place for 1 to 1½ hours, until the dough doubles in size.

NOTE The dough can be wrapped well and frozen, if you wish; thaw in the refrigerator or at room temperature.

This recipe, from Lydecker's next cookbook, is classic comfort food. Serve the stew over crusty bread to soak up every bit of the sauce, which gets its deep flavor from pancetta, shallots and mushrooms.

VEAL STEW WITH MUSHROOMS & PEAS

MAKES 4 SERVINGS

- 3 tablespoons extra-virgin olive oil
- 2 large shallots, finely chopped
- One 2-ounce piece of pancetta, sliced ¼ inch thick and cut into ¼-inch dice
- 10 ounces cremini mushrooms, thinly sliced
- 1½ pounds veal shoulder, cut into 1-inch pieces
- Kosher salt and freshly ground pepper
- 2 tablespoons all-purpose flour
- ½ cup dry white wine
- 1¼ cups chicken stock or low-sodium broth
- ⅓ cup heavy cream
- 1 cup frozen baby peas, thawed
- Four 1-inch-thick slices of crusty white bread, lightly toasted

EDITOR'S WINE CHOICE

Lush, spicy Sicilian red: 2007 Valle dell'Acate Cerasuolo di Vittoria Classico

1. In a very large, deep skillet, heat 2 tablespoons of the olive oil. Add the shallots and pancetta and cook over moderate heat until lightly browned, about 8 minutes. Add the mushrooms and cook until softened, about 8 minutes. Scrape the mushroom mixture into a bowl.

2. In the same skillet, heat the remaining 1 tablespoon of olive oil until shimmering. Season the veal with salt and pepper and cook over moderately high heat, turning once, until browned. Add the flour and cook over moderate heat, stirring, until the veal is coated, about 1 minute. Pour in the wine and cook for 1 minute, scraping up the brown bits from the bottom of the skillet. Add the stock and the mushroom mixture and bring to a simmer. Cover partially and cook over low heat, stirring occasionally, until the veal is tender, about 1 hour. Stir in the cream and peas and cook over moderate heat until the sauce is slightly thickened, about 1 minute. Set the toasts in shallow bowls, spoon the veal stew on top and serve.

MAKE AHEAD The stew can be refrigerated for up to 2 days. Reheat gently before serving.

TONI LYDECKER ONLINE
tonilydecker.com
Seafood alla Siciliana

SEARED SEA BASS WITH
SPICY SOFFRITO, P. 262

STIR

Barbara Lynch with Joanne Smart

This is the debut cookbook from Barbara Lynch, a 1996 FOOD & WINE Best New Chef and owner of a Boston empire that ranges from her flagship No. 9 Park restaurant to a cooking school called Stir. Here she tells her personal story—Irish girl from the projects saved by a home-ec class—and shares her recipes, a sophisticated blend of Italian and French flavors. Her attitude is practical and I'm-here-to-help. For her Orecchiette with Cauliflower, she uses the vegetable's leaves, which usually go to waste. Her sea bass with soffrito (a "secret weapon" of onion, garlic, celery and peppers) comes with seafood-buying tips. Lynch writes: "I remember how starved I was for information as an aspiring chef"; with this book, she shares her hard-won knowledge.

Published by Houghton Mifflin Harcourt, $35

STIR
Barbara Lynch with Joanne Smart

Honey and vinegar make this soffrito appealingly sweet and sour. This dish is all about the soffrito (and the recipe makes extra); any simply prepared chicken, pork or beef will taste great with it.

SEARED SEA BASS WITH SPICY SOFFRITO

SERVES 4

- 1 small white onion, finely chopped
- 1 small carrot, peeled and finely chopped
- 1 celery stalk, peeled and cut into small dice
- ½ yellow bell pepper, seeds removed, finely chopped
- ½ red bell pepper, seeds removed, finely chopped
- ½ green bell pepper, seeds removed, finely chopped
- ½ jalapeño pepper, seeds removed, finely chopped
- 1 large garlic clove, finely chopped
- 3 tablespoons extra-virgin olive oil, plus more for cooking the fish and serving
- 1½ teaspoons sherry vinegar, plus more to taste
- 1½ teaspoons honey
- ¼ teaspoon crushed red pepper flakes, plus more to taste

Kosher salt and freshly ground black pepper

- 4 sea bass fillets, each about 6 ounces
- ¼ cup finely chopped fresh parsley

Fleur de sel (optional)

EDITOR'S WINE CHOICE

Vibrant, citrusy Sauvignon Blanc: 2009 Box O' Birds

In a medium saucepan, combine the onion, carrot, celery, all the peppers, garlic, 3 tablespoons olive oil, vinegar, honey, and crushed red pepper flakes. Season with ½ teaspoon salt and a few grinds of pepper. Cook over medium heat, stirring occasionally, until the liquid in the pan has reduced and the vegetables are very tender, 45 minutes to 1 hour. Season to taste with salt, pepper, red pepper flakes, and vinegar.

To serve, heat 1 to 2 tablespoons olive oil in a large nonstick skillet over medium-high heat. Pat the fillets dry and add them to the pan skin side down. Cook, undisturbed, until lightly browned on one side, about 3 minutes. Gently turn the fish over and cook until just barely firm to the touch, another 3 to 4 minutes, depending on thickness. (If you can't fit them all in one pan with room around each fillet, cook them either in two pans or in batches, transferring them as they cook to a baking sheet and keeping them warm in a 300°F oven.) Season lightly with salt and pepper and serve each fillet skin side up, over a few tablespoons of the warm soffrito. Finish with a drizzle of extra-virgin olive oil, a sprinkling of parsley, and if you like, a pinch of fleur de sel.

Buying the Best Seafood

Use all of your senses when evaluating fish. Most species of lean or white fish should be white and almost translucent, with no discoloration. If you can't touch the fish yourself, ask the person behind the counter to give it a poke; if it doesn't spring back, it means the fish is old and mushy. Finally, ask to smell the fish you plan to buy; it should not smell fishy but should smell fresh and mild.

Once you taste this rich, lusty ragù, it's likely to become your go-to meat sauce. It's stellar tossed with linguine or rigatoni, but it would also be great in a traditional Bolognese-style lasagna.

BUTCHER SHOP BOLOGNESE

MAKES ABOUT 6 CUPS, ENOUGH FOR 1½ POUNDS OF PASTA TO SERVE 8

- 1 tablespoon extra-virgin olive oil
- 1 medium onion, finely chopped
- 1 large celery stalk, finely chopped
- 1 large carrot, finely chopped
- 5 ounces chicken livers, trimmed and finely chopped
- ¼ cup chopped fresh sage

Kosher salt and freshly ground black pepper

- 1½ pounds ground meat, preferably ½ pound each of veal, pork, and lamb
- 1½ cups dry red wine
- 1½ cups chicken broth, preferably Roasted Chicken Stock (recipe follows), or beef broth

One 14½-ounce can (1½ cups) chopped canned tomatoes

- ½ cup chopped fresh basil
- ½ cup heavy cream, or more to taste (optional)

Freshly grated Parmigiano-Reggiano

The "secret" ingredient in this rich, meaty, creamy, traditional-style Bolognese sauce is chicken livers. Finely chopped and combined with the ground meat, they contribute an amazing depth of flavor without making the sauce livery (which means their addition can be our little secret). Though the sauce is delicious using one or two of the ground meats listed, it tastes best with all three; the lamb especially gives it character. This super-easy recipe can be doubled and freezes well. I serve it over homemade tagliatelle or gnocchi, but it's great with dried pasta, too, especially a wider noodle.

Heat the olive oil in a large, deep skillet or Dutch oven over medium heat. Add the onion, celery, and carrot and cook, stirring occasionally, until tender, 8 to 10 minutes. Add the chicken livers and sage, season with a little salt and pepper, and cook, stirring, until the livers lose their red color, 2 to 3 minutes.

Add the ground meat in batches, letting it brown a little before adding more. Season with a pinch of salt and a few grinds of pepper and cook, stirring, until no red or pink color remains. Pour off most of the fat. Add the wine, increase the heat to high, and boil, stirring occasionally to break up any clumps of meat, until the wine is almost gone, 10 to 15 minutes. Add the broth, tomatoes, and basil. Bring to a boil and then lower the heat to a gentle simmer; you should see an occasional bubble but not a boil. Cook, uncovered, until the sauce is thick, dark, and rich,

continued on p. 264

ITALIAN

STIR
Barbara Lynch with Joanne Smart

EDITOR'S WINE CHOICE

**Bright, earthy Nebbiolo:
2004 Marchesi di Grésy
Martinenga Barbaresco**

for at least 1 hour. (You can keep cooking it longer over low heat, and it will only get better; I cook mine for hours at home and dip a piece of bread into the sauce every time I walk by the pot.) Stir in the cream, if using, and simmer for at least another 10 minutes to heat it through; longer is fine.

Serve the sauce over pasta, topped with freshly ground black pepper and grated Parmesan.

MAKE AHEAD The sauce will keep for a couple of days in the refrigerator covered with plastic wrap and freezes beautifully, too. If going right from the hot pot to the freezer, cool the sauce first by putting it in a bowl set over an ice bath in the sink (stir it occasionally) before storing in an airtight container.

ROASTED CHICKEN STOCK

MAKES ABOUT 1 QUART

One 3- to 3½-pound chicken,
    giblets removed
¼ cup vegetable oil
1 carrot, peeled and chopped
1 white onion, chopped
1 celery stalk, peeled and chopped
1 garlic clove, chopped
2 cups dry white wine
1 tablespoon coriander seeds
1 tablespoon black peppercorns
2 bay leaves
2 sprigs fresh parsley
2 sprigs fresh thyme

While my recipes that call for chicken broth can be prepared with good store-bought chicken broth, they will taste a lot better when made with this deeply flavored homemade version. An addition of fresh herbs toward the end of cooking gives the broth a bright flavor.

Cut the breast meat off the chicken (leaving the breastbone behind) and reserve it for another use. Cut off the legs and thighs, too, and reserve them for another use. (You can leave the wings.) Remove any excess fat—a little meat on the bones is welcome—and cut the carcass into 3- to 4-inch pieces.

In a large soup pot, heat the oil over medium-high heat. Add the bones and let them brown well (stir them only every few minutes), about 15 minutes. Add the carrot, onion, celery, and garlic and cook, stirring occasionally, until they, too, are well browned, about 10 minutes. Pour off any excess fat, add the wine, and cook until the wine has reduced by a little more than half. Add 4 quarts water, the coriander, peppercorns, and bay leaves, and bring to a gentle boil. Reduce to a lively simmer and cook until reduced to about 1 quart, occasionally skimming the surface with a ladle; this reducing step can take as long as 2 hours, but you can be doing other things during this time. Add the parsley and thyme and let steep for 5 minutes.

Strain the stock through a fine-mesh strainer before using or storing.

MAKE AHEAD The beauty of stock is that you can make it one day and then use it long after. Freeze it in varying amounts in airtight containers so you can pull out just what you need for a particular recipe.

Using orecchiette is smart here because the small cauliflower florets and pistachios fit perfectly into the little pasta "cups."

ORECCHIETTE WITH CAULIFLOWER

SERVES 6

- ½ cup shelled unsalted pistachios
- 8 tablespoons (1 stick) unsalted butter, cut into pieces
- 1 medium head cauliflower, cut into small florets
- 5 oil-packed anchovies, drained, rinsed, and finely chopped
- 1 garlic clove, finely chopped
- 2 cups chicken broth, preferably Roasted Chicken Stock (p. 265)
- 1 pound orecchiette
- ½ cup chopped fresh parsley
- ¾ cup finely grated Parmigiano-Reggiano, plus more for sprinkling
- ½ teaspoon crushed red pepper flakes, plus more to taste

Kosher salt and freshly ground black pepper
- 6 tablespoons extra-virgin olive oil

Fleur de sel

EDITOR'S WINE CHOICE

Fresh, lemony Italian white: 2008 Fontaleoni Vernaccia di San Gimignano

This recipe is an adaptation of a dish I first had in Sicily, where anchovies are used with abandon. It's a good habit, as they add a salty, earthy flavor without fishiness and really perk up the cauliflower. In Italy, pine nuts, not pistachios, are typically added to a pasta sauce like this one, but I think pistachios are better. Since I don't like to waste the leaves at the base of the cauliflower head, I chop and cook them with the cauliflower.

Heat the oven to 350°F. Spread the pistachios out on a small baking sheet and bake until lightly toasted, about 5 minutes. Once cool, coarsely chop them.

In a large, deep skillet, melt the butter over medium heat until it smells nutty and is golden brown. Add the cauliflower and cook, stirring, for a minute or two. Add the anchovies and garlic and cook, stirring, for another couple of minutes; the anchovies will dissolve into the butter. Add the chicken broth and cook until the cauliflower is tender, about 5 minutes.

Meanwhile, bring a large pot of well-salted water to a boil. Cook the orecchiette until al dente. Reserve ½ cup of the pasta water before draining the pasta. Add the orecchiette, parsley, Parmesan, and crushed red pepper flakes to the cauliflower and stir to combine. Season to taste with salt and pepper. If the pasta seems dry, add a little of the reserved water. Divide among six serving bowls and sprinkle with the toasted pistachios and more red pepper flakes, if desired. Finish with a drizzle of olive oil and pinch of fleur de sel.

This slightly exotic lamb stew is reminiscent of a Moroccan tagine, with its dried fruit and sweet spices. Because it cooks slowly, the lamb becomes ultratender; adding barley turns it into a one-pot meal.

LAMB STEW WITH SWEET POTATOES & BARLEY

SERVES 6

- 1 tablespoon ground cumin
- 1 teaspoon ground ginger
- 1 teaspoon ground cardamom
- ½ teaspoon ground cinnamon
- ½ teaspoon crushed red pepper flakes
- 2 tablespoons grapeseed or canola oil, plus more as needed
- 2 pounds boneless leg of lamb, trimmed of excess fat and sinew, cut into 1- to 2-inch chunks

Kosher salt and freshly ground black pepper

- 2 medium carrots, peeled and diced
- 1 medium onion, diced
- 2 celery stalks, peeled and diced
- 3 garlic cloves, sliced
- 1 cup dry red wine
- 4 cups beef broth
- 15 prunes
- ½ cup raisins, preferably golden
- 1 pound sweet potatoes, peeled and diced
- 1 cup barley

EDITOR'S WINE CHOICE

Cherry-scented, lively Sangiovese: 2007 Le Corti Chianti Classico

AUTHOR'S NOTE

To add color and a burst of flavor, you can top individual servings of this stew with a tiny salad made of lightly dressed whole leaves of fresh, delicate herbs.

Here's everything you would want to eat on a cold winter or early spring evening: lamb, sweet potatoes, and barley simmered in a deep, dark, and rich sauce of red wine and fragrant spices.

In a small bowl, combine the cumin, ginger, cardamom, cinnamon, and red pepper flakes.

Heat a large Dutch oven or similar braising pot over medium-high heat. Add the oil and let it heat up. Add the meat and let it brown very deeply on one side before turning it to brown all sides; this browning step, crucial for great flavor, can take as long as 10 to 15 minutes. Be sure there is space between the pieces or the lamb will steam instead of brown; sear the lamb in batches if necessary.

Transfer the lamb to a platter or baking sheet as it browns and season well with a few pinches of salt and grinds of pepper.

Add a little more oil to the pot, if needed, then add the carrots, onion, celery, and garlic. Season with a good pinch of salt; cook, stirring up the browned bits on the bottom of the pot. Reduce the heat if necessary and cook until the vegetables are lightly browned, 3 to 4 minutes. Add the spice mixture and red wine, stir, and cook over medium heat until the wine has reduced by about half. Add the beef broth; return the lamb to the pot, nestling it into the liquid. Cover the pot with the lid slightly askew; cook over medium-low heat for 1 hour. Add the prunes and raisins, cover, and cook for another 30 minutes. Add the sweet potatoes, barley, and 3 cups water to the pot, cover, and cook until the potatoes, lamb, and barley are tender, another 45 minutes to an hour, adding up to 1 cup more water if needed. Season to taste with salt and pepper. Serve in bowls.

Lynch's gnocchi are superlight and fluffy. As an alternative to baking them in cream, sauté the boiled gnocchi in extra-virgin olive oil until golden, then serve them with the sauce of your choice.

GNOCCHI PARISIENNE

SERVES 6

- 1 cup water
- 5 tablespoons unsalted butter
- ⅓ cup whole milk
- 2½ teaspoons kosher salt
- 1½ teaspoons Dijon mustard
- 1 garlic clove, minced
- ¼ teaspoon Piment d'Espelette or sweet paprika
- Pinch of freshly grated nutmeg
- 2 cups all-purpose flour
- 5 large eggs
- 5 ounces Gruyère cheese, finely shredded (about 2½ cups)
- 2 tablespoons snipped chives
- ¾ cup heavy cream

1. Preheat the oven to 400°F. Bring a large pot of water to a gentle boil.

2. In a medium saucepan, combine the 1 cup water with the butter, milk, salt, mustard, garlic, Piment d'Espelette and nutmeg and bring to a boil. As soon as the mixture boils, add the flour all at once. Beat the dough with a wooden spoon over moderate heat until the flour is fully incorporated and the dough pulls away from the side of the pan. Cook, stirring to dry out the dough, about 30 seconds. Transfer the dough to a large bowl and let cool slightly, about 5 minutes.

3. Beat the eggs into the dough one at a time, beating until each one is fully incorporated before adding the next. Beat in 2 cups of the Gruyère and the chives.

4. Set a bowl of ice water near the stove. Using a large spatula, transfer the gnocchi dough to a piping bag fitted with a ¾-inch round tip. Carefully hold the bag over the pot of gently boiling water and press out the dough, using a small, sharp knife to cut it into 1-inch lengths before it drops into the pot. Simmer the gnocchi for 3 minutes. With a slotted spoon, transfer the gnocchi to the ice water bath to stop the cooking. Drain the gnocchi and transfer to paper towels; pat dry.

5. In a 9-by-13-inch baking dish, arrange the gnocchi in a single layer. Pour the cream on top; sprinkle with the remaining ½ cup of Gruyère. Bake the gnocchi for 20 minutes, until the cream has thickened slightly and the tops are browned. Serve hot.

MAKE AHEAD The gnocchi can be prepared through Step 4 and refrigerated for up to 1 day.

BARBARA LYNCH ONLINE
stirboston.com
barbaralynch.com

CREDITS

DAMGOODSWEET
*Desserts to Satisfy Your
Sweet Tooth, New Orleans Style*
From *DamGoodSweet* by David
Guas and Raquel Pelzel. Text ©
2009 by David Guas. Photographs
© by Ellen Silverman. Reprinted
by permission of The Taunton Press.

AD HOC AT HOME
Excerpted from *Ad Hoc at Home* by
Thomas Keller with Dave Cruz along
with Susie Heller, Michael Ruhlman,
and Amy Vogler. Copyright
© 2009 by Thomas Keller. Used
by permission of Artisan, a division
of Workman Publishing Co., Inc.,
New York. All rights reserved.
Photographs copyright © 2009
by Deborah Jones.

REAL CAJUN
*Rustic Home Cooking from
Donald Link's Louisiana*
Jacket cover and recipes from *Real
Cajun: Rustic Home Cooking from
Donald Link's Louisiana* by Donald
Link with Paula Disbrowe, copyright
© 2009 by Donald Link. Photographs
copyright © 2009 by Chris Granger.
Used by permission of Clarkson
Potter/Publishers, an imprint of the
Crown Publishing Group, a division
of Random House, Inc.

DOWN HOME WITH THE NEELYS
A Southern Family Cookbook
Jacket cover copyright © 2009 by
Alfred A. Knopf, a division of Random
House, Inc., and recipes from *Down
Home with the Neelys: A Southern
Family Cookbook* by Patrick Neely
and Gina Neely with Paula Disbrowe,
copyright © 2009 by Patrick Neely
and Gina Neely. Used by permission
of Alfred A. Knopf, a division of
Random House, Inc. Photographs
copyright © 2009 by Shelly Strazis.

NEW CLASSIC FAMILY DINNERS
From *New Classic Family Dinners*
by Mark Peel with Martha Rose
Shulman. Copyright © 2009 by Mark
Peel. All rights reserved. Photography
© 2009 by Lucy Schaeffer. Reprinted
by permission of John Wiley & Sons,
Inc., Hoboken, New Jersey.

EARTH TO TABLE
*Seasonal Recipes from
an Organic Farm*
Four recipes, three interior photos
and book cover from *Earth to Table:
Seasonal Recipes from an Organic
Farm* by Jeff Crump and Bettina
Schormann. Text copyright © 2009 by
Jeff Crump. Photographs copyright
© 2009 by Edward Pond (except
where noted in the photography
credits). Reprinted by permission
of HarperCollins Publishers and
Random House Canada.

**HUDSON VALLEY
MEDITERRANEAN**
The Gigi Good Food Cookbook
Three recipes, two interior photos,
book cover from *Hudson Valley
Mediterranean* by Laura Pensiero.
Copyright © 2009 by Laura Pensiero.
Reprinted by permission of
HarperCollins Publishers.
Photography by Leonardo Frusteri.

**WHOLE GRAINS
FOR BUSY PEOPLE**
*Fast, Flavor-Packed Meals
and More for Everyone*
Jacket cover and recipes from
Whole Grains for Busy People by
Lorna Sass, copyright © 2009
by Lorna Sass. Photographs
copyright © 2009 by David Prince.
Used by permission of Clarkson
Potter/Publishers, an imprint
of the Crown Publishing Group,
a division of Random House, Inc.

RUSTIC FRUIT DESSERTS
*Crumbles, Buckles, Cobblers,
Pandowdies and More*
Jacket cover and recipes from *Rustic
Fruit Desserts: Crumbles, Buckles,
Cobblers, Pandowdies, and More* by
Cory Schreiber and Julie Richardson,
copyright © 2009 by Cory Schreiber
and Julie Richardson. Photographs
by Sara Remington, copyright ©
2009 by Sara Remington. Used by
permission of Ten Speed Press,
an imprint of the Crown Publishing
Group, a division of Random
House, Inc.

**BOBBY FLAY'S BURGERS,
FRIES & SHAKES**
Jacket cover and recipes from
*Bobby Flay's Burgers, Fries
& Shakes* by Bobby Flay with
Stephanie Banyas and Sally
Jackson, copyright © 2009 by
Boy Meets Grill, Inc. Photographs
copyright © 2009 by Ben Fink.
Used by permission of Clarkson
Potter/Publishers, an imprint
of the Crown Publishing Group,
a division of Random House, Inc.

EMERIL AT THE GRILL
A Cookbook for All Seasons
Four recipes, one subrecipe, two
interior photos, book cover from
Emeril at the Grill by Emeril Lagasse.
Copyright © 2009 by MSLO
Emeril Acquisition Sub LLC. Cover
photograph © 2009 by Steven
Freeman. Reprinted by permission
of HarperCollins Publishers.

SEVEN FIRES
Grilling the Argentine Way
Excerpted from *Seven Fires*
by Francis Mallmann with Peter
Kaminsky. Copyright © 2009
by Francis Mallmann. Used by
permission of Artisan, a division

INDEX

Page numbers in **bold** indicate photographs.

Page numbers in **bold** indicate photographs.

Page numbers in **bold** indicate photographs.

Page numbers in **bold** indicate photographs.

FOOD&WINE
BOOKS

More books from
FOOD & WINE

Annual Cookbook 2010
Over 600 recipes from the world's best cooks—including celebrity chefs like Tom Colicchio, Rick Bayless, Bobby Flay and more.

Cocktails 2010
More than 150 amazing drink and snack recipes from America's most acclaimed mixologists and chefs, plus an indispensable guide to cocktail basics and the country's best nightspots.

Wine Guide 2010
The most up-to-date guide, with over 1,100 recommendations and an easy-to-use food pairing tip sheet.

Available wherever books are sold, or call 1-800-284-4145 or log on to foodandwine.com/books.